T0213074

Communications in Computer and Information Science   683

Commenced Publication in 2007
Founding and Former Series Editors:
Alfredo Cuzzocrea, Dominik Ślęzak, and Xiaokang Yang

More information about this series at http://www.springer.com/series/7899

Anna-Lena Lamprecht (Ed.)

Leveraging Applications of Formal Methods, Verification, and Validation

6th International Symposium, ISoLA 2014
Corfu, Greece, October 8–11, 2014
and 5th International Symposium, ISoLA 2012
Heraklion, Crete, Greece, October 15–18, 2012
Revised Selected Papers

 Springer

Editor
Anna-Lena Lamprecht
Lero - Irish Software Research Center
University of Limerick
Limerick
Ireland

ISSN 1865-0929   ISSN 1865-0937 (electronic)
Communications in Computer and Information Science
ISBN 978-3-319-51640-0   ISBN 978-3-319-51641-7 (eBook)
DOI 10.1007/978-3-319-51641-7

Library of Congress Control Number: 2016961299

Printed on acid-free paper

This Springer imprint is published by Springer Nature
The registered company is Springer International Publishing AG
The registered company address is: Gewerbestrasse 11, 6330 Cham, Switzerland

Preface

Since its initiation in 2004, the International Symposium on Leveraging Applications of Formal Methods, Verification and Validation (ISoLA, see http://isola-conference.org) has been providing a forum for developers, users, and researchers to discuss issues related to the adoption and use of rigorous tools and methods for the specification, analysis, verification, certification, construction, test and maintenance of software systems from the point of view of their different applications domains. ISoLA explicitly aims at being attractive for researchers and practitioners alike, and features a structure of thematically focused sessions consisting of presentations and panel discussions to underline the symposium's intention.

In October 2014, ISoLA celebrated its 10th anniversary at Corfu (Greece). Complementing the different thematically focused research tracks of the main symposium, it hosted for the first time a Doctoral Symposium as a scientific and networking event specifically targeted at young academics. Master and PhD students were invited to participate and to present their research ideas and projects, to discuss them with the scientific community, and to establish collaborations in their field of research. It was very well adopted (by the young researchers as well as by several seniors that attended the sessions) and presented high-quality works on a wide range of topics.

This volume combines the proceedings of the 2014 Doctoral Symposium and "Automata Learning in Practice" tutorial with selected contributions from the "Process-Oriented Geoinformation Systems and Applications" and "Processes and Data Integration in the Networked Healthcare" tracks of the 2012 edition of ISoLA, which were not included in the symposium's on-site proceedings. The collection of papers contained in this volume is the result of a selection and reviewing process that started with a total of 22 contributions. I am very grateful to all those who acted as reviewers for the efforts they put into the selection process and for the valuable feedback they provided, which were essential to ensure high quality content.

November 2016   Anna-Lena Lamprecht

Organization

Symposium Chairs

Tiziana Margaria   Lero - The Irish Software Research Centre, and
Department of Computer Science and Information
Systems, University of Limerick, Ireland

Bernhard Steffen   TU Dortmund University, Germany

Editor

Anna-Lena Lamprecht   Lero - The Irish Software Research Centre,
University of Limerick, Ireland

Reviewers

Giuseppe Airò Farulla	Politecnico di Torino, Italy
Oliver Bauer	TU Dortmund University, Germany
Steve Boßelmann	TU Dortmund University, Germany
Frederik Gossen	Lero - The Irish Software Research Centre, University of Limerick, Ireland
Axel Hessenkämper	GEA Westfalia Separator Group GmbH, Germany
Falk Howar	Clausthal University of Technology, Germany
Malte Isberner	TU Dortmund University, Germany
Marc Jasper	TU Dortmund University, Germany
Anna-Lena Lamprecht	Lero - The Irish Software Research Centre, University of Limerick, Ireland
Maik Merten	Hochschule des Bundes für öffentliche Verwaltung, Germany
Johannes Neubauer	TU Dortmund University, Germany
Maike Paetzel	Uppsala University, Sweden
Tobias Tauterat	University of Stuttgart, Germany

Contents

Processes and Data Integration in the Networked Healthcare

Rehasport: The Challenge of Small Margin Healthcare Accounting

Markus Doedt[1], Thomas Göke[2], Jan Pardo[1], and Maik Merten[1(✉)]

[1] TU Dortmund University, Dortmund, Germany
{markus.doedt,jan.pardo,maik.merten}@tu-dortmund.de
http://www.tu-dortmund.de
[2] sysTeam GmbH, Dortmund, Germany
thomas.goeke@systeam-gmbh.com
http://www.systeam-gmbh.com

Abstract. The paper presents the development of a Web-based accounting system for rehabilitations sports, which, due to the small profit margins, requires a very economical approach, both for its development and for its later use. The development process was therefore driven by simplicity in two dimensions: the accounting process itself was reduced to the minimum under the given legal circumstances, and the software development was clearly guided by total-cost-of-ownership concerns. In particular, standards where taken and artifacts reused wherever possible.

Keywords: Simplicity · Software reuse · Web applications · Accounting · Healthcare · Rehabilitation sports

1 Introduction

It is a new trend in the German healthcare system to actively encourage patients to try to improve their health conditions by changing their lifestyles. Rehasport[1] is one such initiative. It has the goal to educate disabled people or people with a risk of suffering from disability (i.e. everybody in fact) to be more active and to regularly exercise their bodies. This way Rehasports participants should experience the impact of their own contribution to their health, be it for rehabilitation or simply to preserve/improve their health by regular sports exercises. Ideally, they should achieve a better feeling for their body and improve the quality of their lifes in the long term.

A general specification of Reha-sport has been set up by the German association of statutory health insurances together with various associations of Rehasport providers. This general agreement describes, for example, how and how often Reha-sport sessions have to be exercised, who might be certified as a Rehasport provider, and which basic accounting process has to be followed.

---

[1] Rehasport is a German term for rehabilitation sport or rehabilitation training.

© Springer International Publishing AG 2016
A.-L. Lamprecht (Ed.): ISoLA 2012/2014, CCIS 683, pp. 3–18, 2016.
DOI: 10.1007/978-3-319-51641-7_1

For example, for patients with neck or back pain, muscle weakness or too high percentages of body fat, a typical prescription consists of about 50 sessions of Rehasport. The Rehasport patient may take this description to any certified Rehasport provider in order to exercise there free of charge. (S)he only has to confirm participation by signing a special signature form. The Rehasport provider can then send an invoice to the corresponding statutory health insurance together with this signature form and the description in order to get refunded. Organizing this process of accounting for their typically 300–600 patients is quite painful for Rehasport providers, as there are almost 200 different statutory health insurances which need to be treated individually.

In this paper we present the development of a web-based accounting system for rehabilitations sports, which, due to the small profit margins, requires a very economical approach, both for its development and for its later use. The development process was therefore driven by simplicity in two dimension: the accounting process itself was reduced to the minimum under the given legal circumstances, and the software development was clearly guided by total cost of ownership concerns. In particular, standards where taken and artifacts reused wherever possible.

In particular, the paper sketches how the experience with an existing web application called "Rehasportzentrale"[2] influenced the development of the new web application in its goal to simplify the accounting process. Not only was it possible to benefit from the knowledge about the current bottlenecks of "Rehasportzentrale", but also from the wealth of already collected data concerning the rehasports participants, statutory health insurances, prescriptions, and also date, time and signatures for every Rehasport session. As one of its important process optimizations, the new application automates the secure transfer of this data between the involved participants based on strict management of roles and access rights. This does not only simplify the communication process itself, but also the documentation of information flows – a property which is important in case something went wrong.

The development of the new web application was driven by simplicity as a major concern. Of course, the new application should simplify the life of its users, but simplicity of the software itself was also very important:

- The small profit margins required an cost-of-ownership oriented approach, i.e., the application's life-cycle costs need to be considered continuously.
- Time to market was very essential, to exploit the early mover advantage in a new business area.
- Agility of a simple solution was rated higher than perfectionism, concerning coverage issues and beauty. In particular, being able to cover potential future requests was rated higher than a 100% match of todays requirements.

Throughout the paper we will emphasize simplicity as an essential and currently more and more prominent design principle. Its impact on the user side is evident, e.g., from Apple's enormous success with accessible consumer products, and it

---

[2] This roughly translates to "control center for rehabilitation sports".

gradually enters system development, in particular in cases where fast results and flexibility are in the foreground. Here, the so-called 80/20 approach is central, meaning that often 80% of the requirements can be achieved with only 20% of effort[3]. In fact, in system development, the numbers are even more striking, and one could easily speak of 90/10 approaches, as solutions close to current standards can often be realized in very short time, whereas deviations from those standards may be extremely costly. The project described here illustrates the success of such a KISS ("Keep it simple, stupid") approach.

The remainder of the paper is organized as follows. Section 2 presents the initial situation for our project which resulted in the realization of the optimized process described in Sect. 3. The following sections focus on the realization of the software. In particular, Sect. 4 explains what simplicity in this context means and how it can be achieved, while Sect. 5 addresses the concrete implementation by describing which principles and technologies are used and how they are combined. Finally, Sect. 6 presents our conclusions and directions for future work.

2 The Starting Point of the Project

The central idea behind Rehasport is that keeping people healthy is cheaper than curing avoidable diseases, and of course, is much better for the patients – a typical win-win situation. However, this approach comes with quite some administrative workload for the Rehasport providers. They have to do all the bookkeeping, collect signatures of the patients for each training until a number that is sufficient for preparing an account is reached, and send this account to the patients' health insurance (see Fig. 1).

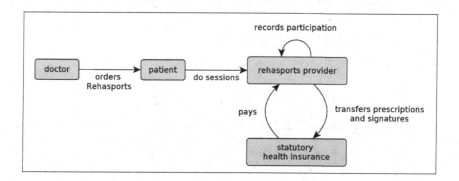

Fig. 1. The accounting process.

This sounds easier as it is, because the up to 600 patients a Reha-Sport provider is serving may have contracts with any of the 200 health insurances in Germany. Moreover, the prices for the sessions vary depending on the kind

---

[3] This rule of thumb is also known as Pareto principle.

of treatment the patient gets. Thus the number and variations of the accounts can be enormous. Also the amount of paper needed for signing (and with it the management of the participation lists) increases with the number of patients. For every patient a single list is needed which consists of several sheets.

This is where sysTeam comes in, a company offering the service to handle this accounting process. sysTeam collects the prescriptions from the doctors, records the signatures at the Rehasport providers, controls when and which accounts can be sent, and handles the whole communication with the statutory health insurances (see Figs. 2 and 3).

That providing this service is profitable for sysTeam is a matter of efficient organization, exploiting synergy coming with the combined treatment of many

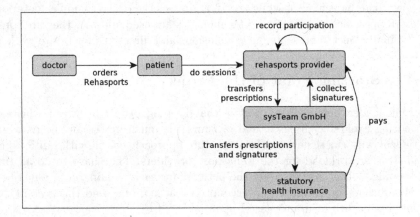

Fig. 2. The accounting process including the offer of sysTeam.

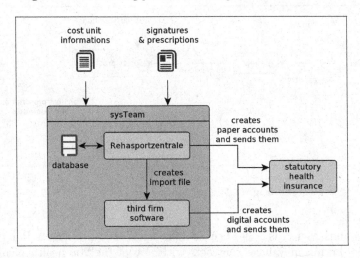

Fig. 3. Interaction of the two applications to create paper and digital accounts at sysTeam.

Reha-Sport providers, and with dedicated process optimization. E.g., sysTeam built a signature pad which can directly record signatures in digital form, which avoids paperwork at the Reha-Sport provider, loss of forms, and other mistakes when manually handling documents in a distributed fashion. In more detail, sysTeam's software "Rehasportzentrale" supports the following process (see Fig. 3):

- Rehasportzentrale collects the signatures entered on the signature pad and stores them in digital form.
- Reha-Sport providers transfer the prescriptions from the doctor and information about the patient (e.g., name, statutory health insurance number etc.) to sysTeam.
- Using Rehasportzentrale, paper accounts are created from this data and are sent to the statutory health insurances.
- Additionally, using third party software, digital accounts are created.
- These digital accounts are then emailed to the statutory health insurances, so that they can start to process the accounts before the paper accounts arrive.

The paper accounts are important for the payment process due to legal requirements. Rehasportzentrale uses two different systems to create the digital and the paper account, a third party system and an own implementation. Both systems have their own data pool. This caused inconsistencies, which needed to be detected and eliminated by means of costly manual reviews. Also the third party system was created for accounting one single Rehasport provider. At present sysTeam is doing the accounting job for about 250 Rehasport providers and for each one a license is needed which lasts for one year. This results in high costs and nearly every day a license has to be updated. Additionally, the third-party software maintains separate databases for each Rehasport provider. To ensure the database of Rehasportzentrale and all third-party software databases are all synchronously up to date, a program checks for changes in the databases. This check takes about 3 days. These are the main motivations to implement a new, comprehensive accounting software.

3 The Optimized Accounting Process

Because of the intricate use of two applications and the resulting high costs and efforts, sysTeam decided to develop a unified application. This application has to store the data to a transactional data source, from where the paper accounts and the digital accounts will be created. Because the application will drive all process steps, only one data source is needed and the synchronous updates wont be needed anymore. Also, the software must be able to be integrated in an existing product. Therefore precise interfaces have to be planned and built. The new software must log what it is doing and give precise feedback in case of errors. The Rehasport providers rely on reliable payment, so delays should be as short as possible. And last, the application architecture should be as simple as possible, allowing for future changes and upgrades.

Furthermore, signatures and prescriptions are collected by the Rehasport providers (as described in Sect. 2), so the software has to import this external information. Also data of the statutory health insurances can be found online (as mandated by German law), and has to be imported. After creating the digital accounts, they must be sent to the statutory health insurances in an encrypted interchange format (also mandated by law). The use of the new software at sysTeam can be seen in Fig. 4.

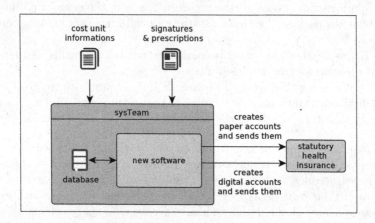

Fig. 4. The use of the new software at sysTeam.

To enable easy access from any computer at sysTeam, the software was realized as web-application. A user management was built to ensure only authorized persons have access to the software. The software runs on a dedicated server with Apache Tomcat and a MySQL database.

Overall, significant cost savings are expected, for instance, due to fewer manual reviews and reduced licensing expenses for third-party software – all while maintaining or improving on the quality of service.

4   Simplicity Patterns

All the way during the development of the accounting software, simplicity has been the main paradigm. Not only should the user process be simple but also the structure of the software as well as its development process. While developing new software there is always an enormous number of decisions to be made. At each decision point the main question we asked ourselves was: "What is the simple way?". But what exactly is that? It should always lead to the lowest *Total Cost of Ownership* (TCO) which amongst others consists of the initial developments costs and license costs for third party software as well as costs resulting from further maintenance in the future. There are several well known paradigms in today's software engineering that target exactly that point.

The principle of *Convention over Configuration* [15] states that there is always a *default* way to do something and as long as this default fits, functionality can be achieved with little or even zero effort. Only if one needs to leave the standard path some additional (but still reasonable) effort is needed. Popular frameworks like Ruby on Rails [7] or Maven [2] and conventions as, e.g., JavaBeans [37] are based heavily on this principle.

The next principle is *You Ain't Gonna Need It* (YAGNI) [22]: one should only implement requested features, without antedating requests. Of course this does not mean that software should not be extensible. Software always has to be developed so that it can be further extended, but not all possible extensions should be implemented right at the beginning.

Another important principle is called *Don't Repeat Yourself* (DRY) [22] which aims at avoiding redundancies wherever possible. What goes hand in hand with this principle is the concept of *reuse* [26]. Once something is implemented, it should never be implemented again. The oldest invention in software engineering for this purpose is probably using something like procedures or functions which can called whenever needed. In the 1990s object orientation improved the possibility of reuse by making it possible to create reusable objects and whole object oriented frameworks [18]. Here one can see that not only is it important to reuse the self developed code, but also code implemented by others. One never wants to "reinvent the wheel". The once so popular *Not Invented Here Syndrome* (NIHS) is frowned upon nowadays. By using frameworks and libraries, one can really stand "on the shoulder of giants". Without third-party software it is nowadays impossible to develop complex software systems. Of course, using third-party software also has got its downsides. What if the vendor of this software does not exist any more and the software is not developed further and/or supported? What if there are bugs that are not fixed? What if the framework does not support the specific feature I need to have now? In all these cases it is important how the frameworks and libraries are used. The emerging software product should be sufficiently modular so that libraries or frameworks can be replaced. Using established standards and appropriate abstraction layers can make this easier. To avoid some kind of "vendor lock-in", third-party software should be embedded utilizing its official interfaces (API) [19], without custom-built workarounds or changes to the internals of the software. If this is not possible, the software is probably not the right choice. A good example for a vendor lock-in resulting from own changes is "customization" of Enterprise Resource Planing (ERP) software. Here a standard *Commercial Off-The-Shelf* (COTS) software is changed until it fits the customer's needs. Unfortunately this can lead to severe problems, e.g., when updating the underlying software base. Replacing a customized software can be very hard or even impossible. The leading paradigm should be "Wrap, don't change!" here.

With the advent of *Service Oriented Architectures* (SOA) [17], the word "reuse" was almost newly defined [16]. Now not only some code can be reused, but concrete instances of running software with defined interfaces: services. These services can then be the building blocks for business processes. For the above-mentioned ERP example that means that now it is not needed any more that the process is in the ERP system. Instead the process controls services provided by the system. When replacing the ERP solution, the process itself can be retained.

Another technique for work reduction is automatic code generation. Code generation can be performed on different sources: 1. source code, 2. specifications/APIs, and 3. abstract models. An example for the first category is Coffee-Script [4], a feature-rich scripting language which is compiled to JavaScript. Code generation from APIs is done, e.g., by stub generation tools of web service frameworks like Axis2 [1] (wsdl2java) or JAX-WS [5] (wsimport). Here Java-stubs are generated from WSDL interface description files. The third kind is probably the most important part and is done in the context of OMG's *Model Driven Architecture* (MDA) [34]. When using code generation one has to be aware of problems resulting from modifying the generated code. If this is allowed a "round-trip" [35] is often desired, which means that each change in the generated code should also result in an appropriate change of the model – a goal that is hard to achieve in practice. In a really *simple* solution the generated code is used as is, with all necessary modifications being done in the source model.

XMDD [27,29,32] (eXtreme Model Driven Design) combines several of the above mentioned techniques and patterns. It helps at defining the above mentioned global processes and its underlying *One Thing Approach* (OTA) [30] ensures that even this can be done in a simple way, because there is always only *one* model for the process and not a huge set of models as, e.g., in UML. In XMDD a simple, hierarchical process model consists of reusable process components called SIBs (Service Independent Building Blocks) [33]. SIBs are coarse grained, parametrized software components that make it possible to call arbitrary services. Using reusable SIBs is a sophisticated technique following the DRY-principle in a service-oriented manner. Besides the code for service invocation, SIBs contain documentation, an icon for visual representation in the process model, and "local check code" which specifies usage rules that are checked at design time for immediate feedback to the model designer. Utilizing the above mentioned *Convention over Configuration* paradigm, SIBs can be created very easily and afterwards be arbitrarily adapted and extended. The model in XMDD is always directly executable by an interpreter or can be used as the source of code generation [24]. The generated code must not be modified, all changes are made on model level. XMDD also deals with skill diversity. For instance, a programmer and a business expert may have different views on what is "simple", which makes it important to establish a "separation of concerns" [23]. In XMDD there are different roles which deal with different matters: the so called "SIB expert" implements the SIBs and the "application expert" (or "business expert") models the process which consists of the SIBs. Of course, both roles have to communicate and interact, e.g., when the application expert formulates requirements for a new SIB.

Another aspect of simplicity is the usability of the software, which is a prerequisite for user acceptance. An important concept to improve usability is the

What You See Is What You Get (WYSIWYG) [20] concept: while editing data, the user will always see what exactly the output will look like. To many people today it is known from different Office-Suites (like Microsoft Office or LibreOffice), where, e.g., text edits are at once presented to the user in a form closely resembling the final printed result. This concept helps the user to understand how data change will influence the resulting output.

The ITSy-Project [31] focused on the topic of simplicity. IT experts and industry practitioners were interviewed about their view on simplicity which led to many insights suggestions for simplicity principles. In [28] they identified five principles, namely *Clearly Defined System Boundaries, Ease of Explanation, Abstraction Layering Refinement, Focus on Simplicity First* and *Don't Build for Failure Containment*. The simplicity patterns described above are well aligned to these principles.

5 Implementation

5.1 Decoupling of Concerns

The software has been designed in accordance to the principles and patterns discussed in Sect. 4. For modularization and separation of concerns, a layer model with four layers is used (see Fig. 5). The topmost layer is the web layer and implemented in Tapestry, an open source web framework of the Apache Software Foundation [3]. The web layer has access to the process layer which is implemented using jABC [36], the reference implementation of the XMDD approach. Here

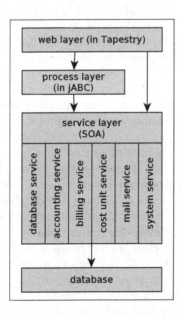

Fig. 5. Layer architectory of the application.

the logic of the application is located. These processes represent the intellectual property of the involved parties. They are thus not "buried" in third party software or hidden in source code, but instead are directly visible to the application experts who are in charge of the business processes. The web layer and the process layer utilize the service layer, which consists of a structured collection of functionality points. Last, the service layer has access to the database layer. Using this architecture, the needs of the application have been separated to different modules, which makes it easier to add new features without touching the existing ones. The processes makes it easy to change the behavior of the application with little to no code changes.

The Tapestry framework used in the web layer supports dynamic and scalable web applications written in Java. It is component-based and uses many techniques that makes it easy to build up a web application. Tapestry follows the "convention over configuration" principle, as well as the DRY-principle. For example, Tapestry brings components that support editing and viewing Java Bean Objects with a single line of code. Also the directories where the pages and components are stored follow a layout convention. As long as the programmer stores the files where Tapestry expects them, the framework will find these files without configuration. For internationalization, Tapestry brings message catalogues. For each page only a properties file with the same name is needed. The file name can be extended by a locale tag (i.e. *en* for English), and Tapestry will automatically read the file with the locale of the calling system. These principles allow for rapid development of feature-rich web applications.

The process layer is built using jABC, a process management framework which supports a high-level layer where the application logic can be graphical arranged. jABC follows the principle of XMDD, and therefore the process model consists of reusable components, the SIBs. While the service layer contains the functionality of the application, the process layer holds the logic of the application. The process layer represents the management process supported by the application. The *Genesys* [24] code generator is used to create Java code from these processes, which is then called by the application. The generated code is one-way – changes to the generated code are not allowed. For behavioral changes the process model is updated, followed by a run of the code generator, avoiding round-trip problems.

The service layer has a number of services that contain the functionality of the application. Architecturally, the service layer follows the SOA as described in Sect. 4. All functionality has been separated into service interfaces, each containing associated concerns. For example, there is a database service for database calls, an import service which contains all functionality for importing data, an accounting service which contains every functionality for creating the account PDF files, and so on. The services are independent, so changes to one service do not affect the other ones. If technical things change, e.g., the way the account data is calculated, only the single service *accounting service* must be edited.

In summary, the service-oriented and strictly layered architecture with the XMDD process at its center lead to a piece of software which is prepared for future change requests. This is achieved by the application of a simple process model (see *One Thing Approach* in Sect. 4) which serves on the on hand as a documentation for the business expert and on the other hand at the same time as the implementation of the software. Using an directly executable process model leads to an always up-to-date process documentation and an agile development process especially in the context of maintenance.

5.2   Using External Knowledge

For many technical challenges that arised during the development of the new application, solutions in the form of ready-to-use third-party software were available. Using this knowledge helps creating complex software in a reasonable time frame. In each case only "glue code" is needed to connect these services to the XMDD process. If sometime in the future a third party component is to be replaced, this is easily possible with only few changes to the implementation of the building blocks (SIBs) the XMDD processes are composed of. In this section some examples are given where third-party software is used to provide essential services.

Object Relational Mapper: The application needs a reliable high-performance mechanism for storing and retrieving data. Relational databases such as MySQL are in widespread use to provide this functionality. Communication with databases is commonly done by preparing SQL statements or by using an *object relational mapper* (ORM) that maps data objects (so-called *entities*) to a relational data model, generating corresponding SQL statements. In this application the Hibernate [8] ORM was used, rendering the task of manually preparing SQL statements unnecessary and lifting database programming onto a high level of abstraction. If data structures changes, only the corresponding entities must be updated accordingly. Using the entities for Hibernate is a good example showing the realization of the DRY-principle as described in Sect. 4.

Import of EDIFACT-Files: Due to German law, the data of the statutory health insurances can be found online [9] in *Electronic Data Interchange For Administration, Commerce and Transport* (EDIFACT) format. EDIFACT is a text-format where data is given in value separated lines with a line-separator at the end. Also multiple lines can be grouped to show their togetherness.

The EDIFACT files have to be parsed for transferring them to database. Developing a reliable EDIFACT parser would have consumed a lot of time, thus an existing EDIFACT parser was chosen that converts EDIFACT files to XML files. The resulting XML files are transferred into object-oriented data structures by using JAXB [6], a Java XML Binding Framework. The whole process how an EDIFACT file is parsed can be seen in Fig. 6.

Using external software made it easy to parse EDIFACT files – only a few lines of code had to be written, resulting in a very quick implementation of a complex functionality.

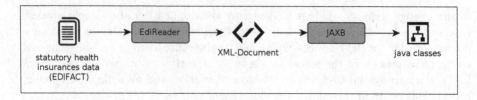

Fig. 6. The way EDIFACT files are parsed using external software

Creating Portable Documents: The accounts must be saved in a document format that can easily be printed and which can be read on various computers. The *Portable Document Format* (PDF) is able to fulfill these requirements. As PDF is a complex binary format, it is a logical decision not to write the document file ourselves. For Java a handful of framework exists which allow to create PDFs and the way they work is very similar. Either they allows to create single pages by drawing to a canvas (like Suns Graphics2D framework), or they convert HTML files to a PDF document so only HTML files have to be created.

These solutions, however, have limitations regarding the quality of the document layout. Thus the account PDFs are created using LaTeX [10], a document preparation system. We created a template for the LaTeX file, which is filled with the necessary data using the template framework Apache Velocity [14] whenever a document has to be created. This filled template then is the input for the LaTeX building process. For layout changes only the template has to be edited. No code changes are necessary and templates can be changed without halting the application.

This usage of third party software allows us to create PDF files with little effort. Obviously, this approach only works on systems with LaTeX installed. In our case, because the application is a server application and we have full server control, this is not a real problem.

Export in PKCS#7-Format: The statutory health insurances instruct encryption of transmitted data to ensure privacy [12]. Therefore they offer X509-standard certificates for all of their members [11]. The data first has to be signed with the sender certificate to ensure the correct sender, and afterwards must be encrypted so that only the receiver is able to decrypt. This has to be done following the *Public Key Crypto Standard* in version 7 (PKCS#7) [21,25]. In this standard, the data will be signed with a SHA hash generated including the sender certificate and then transfered to a data structure in the *Abstract Syntax Notation* (ASN). The ASN is an abstract data structure which has many ways for representation. Here, the *Distinguished Extension Rules* (DER) are needed, which is a byte encryption. This structure will be encrypted using the Triple DES Encryption standard with a randomly generated key. Afterwards this key will be encrypted with the RSA public key of the receivers certificate. The encrypted signed data and the encrypted key will then be encapsulated with a data structure called *envelope* which is also in ASN (and represented in DER).

It is easy to see that generating PKCS#7-compliant data involves a complex series of steps that need to be implemented with utmost care. This complexity makes maintaining a newly-developed implementation undesirable. Thus a library was chosen (bouncycastle [13]) which can directly convert a data stream to an ASN data structure following the PKCS#7 standard. Therefore only a few lines of codes are needed to create a signed and encrypted data stream in the required format.

5.3 Processes with jABC

While the service layer holds all services, the logic of the application is implemented in processes, calling services in the service layer. The processes follow the principle of XMDD as described in Sect. 4 and are designed using jABC, a process modeling framework.

In the application each process is encapsulated by a starting class. This class has a method that initializes the process execution context with the necessary data and then calls the process. This encapsulation was necessary to have a well-defined entry point for each process without editing the code generated from the processes, which would have violated the paradigm of never editing generated code. This approach also gives the process a stable service-like interface.

In Fig. 7, the process driving accounting cycles can be seen. In this process, first the billable prescriptions are collected. If a non empty set was gathered, the real accounting can start, otherwise the process will end. On the real accounting, first some database entries will be created. Then for each prescription the

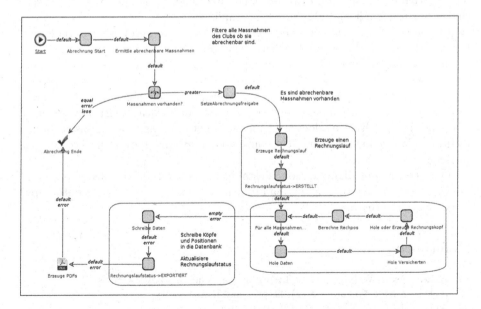

Fig. 7. A process implementing an accounting cycle

accounting will be arranged. After that, the collected data is written to database and the account PDF files are created before the end of the process.

This example shows how the services are assembled to implement a business process. The graphical modeling makes it easy to discuss the business logic and make changes. If, for example, the accounts should also be created as XML or CSV files, only a service which converts the accounts to these formats has to be created and integrated into this process.

5.4   Usability

The frontend of the software follows the principle of *WYSIWYG* as described in Sect. 4: on every data change the PDF file for the paper account will be newly created and presented to the user. This guarantees that the user is given direct feedback on how his editing will affect the result.

6   Conclusion and Future Work

In this paper we presented a case study in which a web application for the accounting of rehabilitation sports has been implemented with the focus on "simplicity". This software simplifies the life of its users and itself is structured following principles of simplicity.

From a software engineering point of view especially the XMDD approach is of interest because it lead to an easy to maintain piece of software which documents itself and at the same time orchestrates all third-party-software in a service-oriented manner. This makes it possible to easily adapt to, e.g., market changes or new challenges due to legal compliance.

By means of a service oriented web application the accounting process for Rehasport could be developed for simplicity, efficiency and time and cost saving for all parties involved. However, apart from Rehasport, there are further approaches for future work. Today, in addition to the digital accounting process described in this article, paper copies of prescriptions and signature forms have to be sent together with a paper invoice to the statutory health insurances where the paper is digitalized by document management systems again. Consequently, future work should be spent on a continuous digitalization of the accounting process.

Once continuous digitalization is established in the field of Rehasport, there are various more areas of application in the health care system like physiotherapy or occupational therapy.

References

1. Apache Axis2 Website (2012). http://axis.apache.org/axis2/java/core/
2. Apache Maven Website (2012). http://maven.apache.org/
3. Apache Tapestry Website (2012). http://tapestry.apache.org/
4. CoffeeScript Website (2012). http://coffeescript.org/

5. JAX-WS Reference Implementation Website (2012). http://jax-ws.java.net/
6. JAXB Website (2012). http://jaxb.java.net/
7. Ruby on Rails Website (2012). http://rubyonrails.org
8. Hibernate Website (2013). http://www.hibernate.org/
9. Kostenträger-Dateien der sonstigen Leistungserbringer (2013). http://www.gkv-datenaustausch.de/leistungserbringer/sonstige_leistungserbringer/kostentraegerda teien_sle/kostentraegerdateien.jsp
10. Latex website (2013). http://www.latex-project.org/
11. Öffentiches Schlüsselverzeichnis der sonstigen Leistungserbringer (2013). ftp://trust.itsg.de/dale/
12. Security-Schnittstelle für den Datenaustausch im Gesundheitswesen (2013). http://www.gkv-datenaustausch.de/standards_und_normen/sicherheitsverfahren/ sicherheitsverfahren.jsp
13. The Legion of the Bouncy Castle (2013). http://www.bouncycastle.org/
14. Apache Sofware Founcation: Apache Velocity Website (2012). http://velocity. apache.org/
15. Chen, N.: Website about "Convention over Configuration" (2012). http:// softwareengineering.vazexqi.com/files/pattern.html
16. Dan, A., Johnson, R.D., Carrato, T.: Soa service reuse by design. In: Proceedings of the 2nd International Workshop on Systems Development in SOA Environments, SDSOA 2008, pp. 25–28. ACM, New York (2008). http://doi.acm.org/10.1145/ 1370916.1370923
17. Erl, T.: Service-Oriented Architecture: Concepts, Technology, and Design. Prentice Hall PTR, Upper Saddle River (2005)
18. Fayad, M., Schmidt, D.C.: Object-oriented application frameworks. Commun. ACM 40(10), 32–38 (1997). http://doi.acm.org/10.1145/262793.262798
19. Fowler, M.: Public versus published interfaces. Softw. IEEE 19(2), 18–19 (2002)
20. Goldberg, A.: A History of Personal Workstations. Addison-Wesley Publishing Company, New York (1988)
21. Housley, R.: Cryptographic message syntax (CMS). Technical report (2009)
22. Hunt, A., Thomas, D.: The Pragmatic Programmer: From Journeyman to Master. Addison-Wesley Longman Publishing Co., Inc., Boston (1999)
23. Hürsch, W.L., Lopes, C.V.: Separation of concerns. Technical report (1995)
24. Jörges, S., Margaria, T., Steffen, B.: Genesys: service-oriented construction of property conform code generators. Innov. Syst. Softw. Eng. 4, 361–384 (2008). doi:10. 1007/s11334-008-0071-2
25. Kàliski, B.: PKCS #7: cryptographic message syntax. Technical report (1998)
26. Krueger, C.W.: Software reuse. ACM Comput. Surv. 24(2), 131–183 (1992). http://doi.acm.org/10.1145/130844.130856
27. Kubczak, C., Jörges, S., Margaria, T., Steffen, B.: eXtreme model-driven design with jABC. In: Proceedings of the Tools and Consultancy Track of the 5th European Conference on Model-Driven Architecture Foundations and Applications (ECMDA-FA), CTIT Proceedings, vol. WP09-12, pp. 78–99. CTIT (2009)
28. Margaria, T., Floyd, B., Steffen, B.: It simply works: simplicity and embedded systems design. In: 2011 IEEE 35th Annual Computer Software and Applications Conference Workshops (COMPSACW), pp. 194–199, July 2011
29. Margaria, T., Steffen, B.: Continuous model-driven engineering. Computer 42, 106–109 (2009)
30. Margaria, T., Steffen, B.: Business process modelling in the jABC: the one-thing approach. In: Handbook of Research on Business Process Modeling. IGI Global (2009)

31. Margaria, T., Steffen, B.: Simplicity as a driver for agile innovation. Computer **43**(6), 90–92 (2010)
32. Margaria, T., Steffen, B.: Service-orientation: conquering complexity with XMDD. In: Hinchey, M., Coyle, L. (eds.) Conquering Complexity, pp. 217–236. Springer, London (2012)
33. Margaria, T., Steffen, B., Reitenspieß, M.: Service-oriented design: the roots. In: Benatallah, B., Casati, F., Traverso, P. (eds.) ICSOC 2005. LNCS, vol. 3826, pp. 450–464. Springer, Heidelberg (2005). doi:10.1007/11596141_34
34. Mellor, S.J., Scott, K., Uhl, A., Weise, D.: Model-driven architecture. In: Bruel, J.-M., Bellahsene, Z. (eds.) OOIS 2002. LNCS, vol. 2426, pp. 290–297. Springer, Heidelberg (2002). doi:10.1007/3-540-46105-1_33
35. Sendall, S., Küster, J.: Taming model round-trip engineering (2004). http:// citeseerx.ist.psu.edu/viewdoc/summary?doi=10.1.1.94.7515
36. Steffen, B., Margaria, T., Nagel, R., Jörges, S., Kubczak, C.: Model-driven development with the jABC. In: Bin, E., Ziv, A., Ur, S. (eds.) HVC 2006. LNCS, vol. 4383, pp. 92–108. Springer, Heidelberg (2007). doi:10.1007/978-3-540-70889-6_7
37. Sun Microsystems: JavaBeans Specification (1997). http://www.cs.vu.nl/~eliens/ documents/java/white/beans.101.pdf

Process-Oriented Geoinformation Systems and Applications

Design and Implementation of Data Usability Processor into an Automated Processing Chain for Optical Remote Sensing Data

Erik Borg[1], Bernd Fichtelmann[1(✉)], Christian Fischer[2],
and Hartmut Asche[3]

[1] German Aerospace Center, German Remote Sensing Data Center,
Kalkhorstweg 53, 17235 Neustrelitz, Germany
{Erik.Borg,Bernd.Fichtelmann}@dlr.de
[2] German Aerospace Center, German Remote Sensing Data Center,
Münchner Str. 20, 82234 Wessling, Germany
C.Fischer@dlr.de
[3] Department of Geography, University of Potsdam,
Karl-Liebknecht-Strasse 24/25, 14476 Potsdam, Germany
gislab@uni-potsdam.de

Abstract. Diverse anthropogenic impacts will trigger worldwide environmental and social problems as e.g. climate change or social transformation processes. To observe these processes current information about status, direction of development and spatial or temporal dynamics of the processes are required. As the demand for current environmental information is increasing, earth observation (EO) and remote sensing (RS) techniques are moving to the focus of interest.

Generation and dissemination of RS based information products for e.g. time-critical applications can only be guaranteed by state-of-the-art concepts for data processing. This can be realized either by cumbersome and thus expensive interactive processing or by setting-up development and implementation of automated data processing infrastructure. In both cases information about data quality is important for the pre-processing and value adding processing steps. This contribution is focussed on a processor for automated data usability assessment which can be integrated into an automated processing chain adding information valuable for the user.

Keywords: Remote sensing · Processing chain · Data quality · LANDSAT

1 Introduction

Increasing scarcity of natural resources, such as fresh water or fertile soils, coupled with conflicting man-made pressures on land use results in potential risks for a sustainable development of natural environment and thus requires a careful use of limited resources. Hence, it is necessary to balance the different user requirements in order to

© Springer International Publishing AG 2016
A.-L. Lamprecht (Ed.): ISoLA 2012/2014, CCIS 683, pp. 21–37, 2016.
DOI: 10.1007/978-3-319-51641-7_2

limit, and if possible, to reduce the increasing pressure on environment and its different land-cover and land-use classes. The knowledge of environmental parameters and the availability of geographic information are important prerequisites if progress is to be achieved on this issue successfully. To respond to global land-use conflicts the European Union (EU) and European Space Agency (ESA) have jointly initiated the COPERNICUS-programme, which is aiming in the development and provision of fundamental, accurate and reliable geo-information services based on RS data products and ancillary spatial data (e.g. in-situ-information) [1]. To establish a geo-data database a variety of state-of-the-art remote sensing (RS) technologies, including data from optical and radar satellite systems, have to be utilised.

Many geo- and biophysical parameters that are required for monitoring and/or modelling of environmental processes can only be derived by using optical RS. However, the quality of optical data depends substantially on the weather conditions at the time of data recording.

In cases of cloud-obscured optical data, interactive processing of sub-optimal datasets by an operator becomes inevitable. However, operator-based image evaluation and processing to extract geo- and biophysical parameters is time-consuming, requires considerable expertise, manpower, and, although defined visual interpretation defaults were met, each operator develops an own interpretation and assessment model. Thus, the results obtained for a given image can vary and under certain circumstances and the results are often not comparable. Especially, since the interactive visual data evaluation is very expensive, in many cases only cloud-free or nearly cloud-free data are preferred for an interactive data processing.

By using only optimal cloud-free data, the requirements of the COPERNICUS initiative for delivering value-added information products and environmental geo-services based on area-wide RS data cannot be fulfilled. This is only possible if all RS data, inclusive sub-optimal data, are processed. However, if those data are processed interactively the i. quality of value-added products cannot be standardised because by subjectivity of operators, and ii. manpower and time requirements of processing will significantly increase the production costs.

A solution for this problem is the development of an automated processing chain for sub- and /or optimal data at acceptable time and costs. This ensures the i. generation of usable quality products of bio- and geophysical information, ii. provision of area-wide value-added products for a given time or period, and iii. setup and control of automatic processing by choosing appropriate satellite data processing modules.

Relevant control parameters may include technical system parameters (gain and offset) as well as data acquisition parameters (acquisition time (scene centre scan time and/or start and stop of scan), geographical corner and/or centre coordinates, and sun azimuth and elevation angle of scene centre). Thus, meta-information on data quality is particular an important control parameter, for either choosing high-quality data for expensive interactive thematic processing or for event-driven control of automated pre-processing and thematic processing. This contribution focuses on data quality parameter, that directly can be assessed from a given RS dataset and either can be expressed in terms of the cloud cover index[1] or the data usability index[2].

This paper deals with a data usability processor as part of an automatic processing chain. The processor supports data error assessment, calculation of geographical coordinates, and local time for real solar conditions of all image pixels. Furthermore, the provision of land-water information for quality assessment, the determination of cloud and haze coverage is shown, and the influence of cloud and haze distribution to data quality is discussed.

2 Materials and Methods

2.1 Data Basis

For developing the processing chain presented here 2,957 JPEG-compressed quick-look-data[3] with corresponding metadata[4] from the period of 2000 to 2003 have been used. A description of the preparation of the quick-look-data is given in [2, 3]. The procedure results in resampled bands of a ground resolution of 180 m and by using a JPEG-compression ratio of 10:1 [2] to minimize the storage volume. Although the level of compression depends on the image content of a RS scene, this represents a JPEG quality metric Q-factor of 35 [4].

2.2 Processing Chain

The European receiving station network for LANDSAT-7 comprises stations in Maspalomas (Spain), Kiruna (Sweden), Matera (Italy), and Neustrelitz (Germany).

These stations guarantee the receiving and storage of data on behalf of ESA and data processing is carried out in order of EURIMAGE [6][5]. Figure 1 shows a block diagram of the LANDSAT ground segment operated by the German Remote Sensing Data Center (DFD). The received data are processed and stored with subsequent metadata generated during the receiving phase [8]. The interactive processing step in the automatic processing chain is highlighted in red. At this point, data assessment is completed visually by interpreters using quick-look-data. The assessment framework for the interpretation was provided by ESA [9], covering the range from 0 = perfect usable to 90 = unusable and addresses criteria such as: i. artefacts (90 = unusable), ii. estimated haze, clouds, and cloud shade, iii. assessment of cloud distribution, iv. differentiation of clouds covering land or water, and v. estimation of data usability

---

[1] *Cloud Cover Degree:* Ratio of cloud pixels to total pixels of an unit (e.g. complete scene or quadrant of a scene).

[2] *Data usability:* Combination of cloud cover and cloud distribution as well as data errors.

[3] *Quick-look data* are preview images derived from original remote sensing data.

[4] *Metadata* describe remote sensing data (e.g. satellite mission, orbit, track, frame).

[5] LANDSAT-7/ETM + data receiving were stopped at the end of 2003 [7].

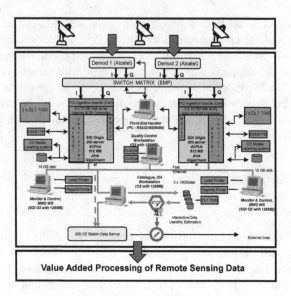

Value Added Processing of Remote Sensing Data

Fig. 1. Block diagram of the LANDSAT ground segment - red highlighted: interactive data usability assessment (adopted and changed from [5]). (Color figure online)

for land applications. The generated metadata and assessment results are then transferred to ESA [8].

3   Data Usability Processor for a Processing Chain

In addition to geographical and atmospheric data correction [10, 11] and the so called value adding (Fig. 2, left part) the development of the data usability processor for optical RS data can be integrated into the automated value added processing chain (adopted and changed from [12, 13]) (Fig. 2, right part).

Metadata[6] generated for the quick-look of Landsat-7/ETM+ data are essential to control the processing steps and for internal data transfer to the processor. The first processing step is to analyse the quick-look-data with respect to data errors, such as scan mirror errors, missing pixels, lines and areas [14].

If an erroneous data set is identified the data processing is terminated, otherwise the data is subjected to further processing by the cloud cover assessment (CCA) module, which is the processor core (right side in Fig. 2) and includes calibration, referencing to map in a usable projection and further classification by using sub-modules. The calibration module uses radiometric gain and offset, corner coordinates (based on preliminary Two-Line-Elements of satellite orbit) of the scene as well as equator crossing time to calculate at least sun elevation angle. These parameters are a pre-condition to

---

[6] *Meta-information:* Contain further information on remote sensing data (e.g. satellite mission, orbit, track, frame number, etc.).

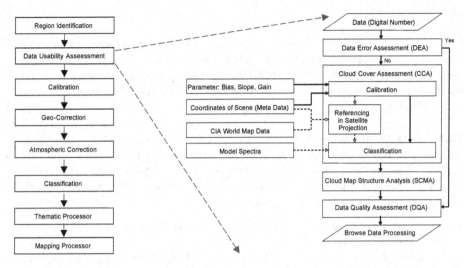

Fig. 2. Schematic diagram of a processing chain to derive value-added products (left) and integration of the developed data usability processor (right)

transform 8-bit observed uncalibrated raw data quantized in units of digital number (DN) to Top-of-the-Atmosphere (TOA) spectral radiance and after that into TOA reflectance for each pixel of optical bands, respectively, thermal band into surface temperature.

In the next processing step a land-water map is generated for the region of image data using geographical scene coordinates. The result of inverse geo-referencing of the land-water map to satellite image/quick-look data is subsequently used to control the cloud-haze-classification with respect to the background (land, water), and to optimise structure analysis in the quality assessment module (DQA).

For LANDSAT different classification algorithms are available [15, 16] facilitating the selection of an optimal processing module according to the target characteristics or geographic location.

The cloud-haze-mask allows the assessment of cloud cover degree of an image and it serves as an input for the subsequent cloud map structure analysis (SCMA). This module computes cloud distribution parameters for an assessment unit[7] (like a complete scene or a quadrant). The cloud cover and cloud distribution information are quality parameters for further processing [17].

These quality parameters are combined by using DQA in order to generate a data usability measure, whereas the cloud cover degree is a principal quality criteria and the cloud cover distribution is considered as an additional quality criteria to refine the data usability. Only this auxiliary criterion makes it possible to estimate the size of the usable image area [2].

---

[7] *Assessment unit:* scene, quadrant.

3.1   Pre-processing

Pre-processing of the data is an essential processing steps of the processor introduced here. The pre-processing subroutines include the following aspects (i) data error assessment, (ii) calibration, and (iii) transformation of topographic information into the original satellite image data. A short description of the different sub-processors is given in the following sections.

3.1.1   Data Error Assessment

According to ESA requirements [9], received imagery that is considered erroneous is excluded from further processing and is labelled as not further useable. Therefore, a reliable method for data error detection was developed [13]. The features used to distinguish both classes with high certainty are:

- Detection of erroneous lines or data sections showing only poor correlation with neighbouring undisturbed lines.
- Detection of erroneous image parts, lines or a number of pixels with *radiance = 0* in units of digital number (DN), characterizing the data as being unusable.

The preliminary test on selected erroneous LANDSAT-7/ETM+JPEG-compressed quick-look data have showed, that:

- missing lines cannot be identified with a high degree of confidence at very low sun angles,
- artefacts caused by the JPEG-compression led to a variety of false indications,
- computing time for determination of erroneous data sets is relatively high.

Therefore, a simplified method was developed which is based on the acceptance that erroneous pixel are characterized by *radiance = 0* in units of DN. The total number of such pixels is determined per line and tested against a threshold value of 10 pixels[8].

However, to minimize false indications, a threshold value was empirically derived for the identification of erroneous scenes. Moreover, the criterion 2 (*radiance = 0* in units of DN) proved to be adequate for the discrimination of disturbed and undisturbed data sets.

After data error analysis, usable data sets are provided to the next processing step while the other data are selected and labelled as non-usable.

3.1.2   Calibration

Calibration and transformation of LANDSAT-7/ETM+ data to TOA reflectance ρ and to effective at-sensor brightness temperature T $[K]$ is described in detail by the LANDSAT-handbook [14]. Additional aspects which have to be considered for calibration is given by [17], computing planetary top of atmosphere reflectance ρ_p of band k based on digital number of a pixel (DN) [18, 19]. The relation to approximate Earth-Sun-distance d is given by [20].

---

[8] It has been shown that a threshold value of 10 is optimal because single zero-pixels are often caused by JPEG compression and were no data problem.

The transformation of pixel radiance in units of *DN* into planetary top of atmosphere reflectance ρ_p in a specified band k can be calculated by using Eq. (1) [14, 15, 18, 19]:

$$\rho_p = (\pi L(\lambda_k)d^2)/(E_S(\lambda_k)cos\Theta_S) \tag{1}$$

with: $L(l_k) = Gain(\lambda_k) * QCAL + Bias(\lambda_k)$, $L(l_k)$ spectral radiance at sensor's aperture $[W/(m^2 sr\mu m)]$, Gain in $W/(m^2 sr\mu m)/DN$, QCAL the quantized calibrated pixel value in *DN*, *Bias* in $[W/(m^2 sr\mu m)]$, $E_S(\lambda_K)$ mean exoatmospheric solar irradiance $[W/(m^2 \mu m)]$, d Earth-Sun distance [*Astronomical Units*], and Θ_S solar zenith angle [*degrees*].

The transformation of spectral radiance in units of DN of thermal band 6 (wavelength: 10.4 μm to 12.5 μm) into at-sensor temperature T [K] can be calculated by using Eq. (2).

$$T = K_2/ln((K_1/L(l) + 1) \tag{2}$$

with: L_λ spectral radiance at the sensor's aperture $[W/(m^2 sr\mu m)]$, K_1 calibration constant 1 $[666,09 W/(m^2 sr\mu m)]^9$, K_2 calibration constant 2 $[1282,71\ K]^{10}$.

3.1.3   Calculation of All Pixel Coordinates

The use of the solar zenith angle in Eq. (1) assumes at first that the geographic coordinates of all pixels are available. But only the corner coordinates of the scene are given for Landsat imagery, thus the coordinates for each individual pixel have to be calculated first. Additionally, the coordinates can be used to select topographic information for further data analyses.

The satellite orbit can be characterized in a static (non-rotation of Earth) geographical system Σ' using a reference track in a satellite system Σ, in which the track can be described only by length λ, while the latitude φ is 0 in every case. This satellite system is rotated by an angle $\delta = (180° - \iota)$ (ι = inclination of the real orbit and reference satellite orbit in Σ') against the x-axis, which crosses exactly by ($\varphi = 0$, $\lambda = 0$), opposite to the geographical system.

The advantage of an equatorial orbit in system Σ is based on the fact that for a corresponding satellite image the distance between two points can be calculated with the relation (Eq. 3), assuming a spherical Earth piecemeal between the corner coordinates:

$$\varphi_1 = \varphi_0 + i\Delta\varphi$$
$$\lambda_1 = \lambda_0 + j\Delta\lambda \tag{3}$$

---

[9] LANDSAT-handbook: chapter 9.2.4, Table 9.2 ETM+ Thermal Constants.
[10] LANDSAT-handbook: chapter 9.2.4, Table 9.2 ETM+ Thermal Constants.

where: $\Delta\varphi$ and $\Delta\lambda$ are the pixel size in latitude and longitude, respectively, and i and j are the distance of the two pixels in columns and lines.

The transformation of the coordinates φ and λ of system Σ into coordinates φ' and λ' of the geographical system Σ' is described by Eq. (4), where $r = r'$ [21]:

$$\begin{aligned}
\cos\varphi' \cos\lambda' &= \cos\varphi \cos\lambda \\
\cos\varphi' \sin\lambda' &= \cos\delta \cos\varphi \sin\lambda - \sin\delta \sin\varphi \\
\sin\varphi' &= \sin\delta \cos\varphi \sin\lambda - \cos\delta \sin\varphi
\end{aligned} \tag{4}$$

In each case, since the latitude of reference track is identical to geographical latitude of the real track in the geographical system, φ' can be considered as known. However, the coordinates of the track in Σ, defined by $\varphi = 0$, $\sin\varphi = 0$, and $\cos\varphi = 1$, are not given. But the coordinates for UL, UR, LR, and LL are known in the system Σ'. UL and LL are on parallel small circle track to satellite track, neglecting Earth rotation. The difference to longitude of LL is given by Earth rotation and will be calculated in one of the next steps.

The respective 4 geographical latitudes define the reference track in geographical coordinates. The corner coordinates on the left side of Eq. (4) and the angle δ on the right sight are known. The coordinates on the right side have to be determined to use at least Eq. (3) for determination of all pixel coordinates of the scene in system Σ. After that all coordinates in Σ can be transferred into the coordinate system Σ'. At least the deviation to the real track in the rotating system has to be determined.

The knowledge of the respective longitudes λ' is not necessary for the terms in line 3 of Eq. (4). The transformation of a small circle is sufficient for segmentation of an image in constant longitudes and latitudes sections. However, to transform the two left corner coordinates within Eq. (5) $\varphi = \varphi_G$ has to calculated as a prerequisite.

$$\lambda_k = arcsin[(sin\varphi_k - cos\delta sin\varphi_G)/(sin\delta cos\varphi_G)]; \quad \text{with } k = UL, LL \tag{5}$$

φ_G is given as latitude in the satellite system Σ and is the spherical distance between small circle and great circle, which represents the reference track. However, this distance is the same in every system Σ'. It is exactly half of the spherical distance of the two upper corner pixels which are located on the great circle. Pass the great circle (orthodrome) on a globe the points $A(\varphi_A, \lambda_A)$ and $B(\varphi_B, \lambda_B)$ the spherical distance α can be calculated to:

$$\alpha = arccos[sin\varphi_A - sin\varphi_B + cos\varphi_A cos\varphi_B cos(\lambda_B - \lambda_A)]; \quad A = UL, LL; B = UR, LR$$

For both pairs A, B the result is same with:

$$\varphi_G = \pm\alpha/2 \tag{7}$$

Knowing the difference of both longitudes when solving Eq. (5) for UL and LL and the corresponding line number n the line spacing $\Delta\lambda$ in Eq. (3) can be computed for the scene by Eq. (8).

$$\Delta\lambda = [(\lambda^0_{UL} - \lambda'_{UL})/n]; \quad \text{with } n = \text{ line number} \tag{8}$$

The distance $\Delta\varphi$ (Eq. 3) between image elements of a line can be calculated using the pre-calculated spherical distance α for the borderline of the swath and the number of m image elements (columns) using Eq. (9):

$$\Delta\varphi = \alpha/m; \quad \text{with } m = \text{ column number} \tag{9}$$

The use of m and n assume, that under specific cases the coordinates of the *UL* corner corresponds the upper left corner of the *UL* pixel. In this case, it is necessary to include $\Delta\varphi$ /2 and $\Delta\lambda$ /2 in Eq. (3). If the centre of the *UL* pixel is given as upper left corner of the scene $(n-1)$ and $(m-1)$ have to be used in Eqs. (8) and (9).

A prerequisite for applying Eq. (9) is a scanning geometry with constant distance between line elements in Σ. In other case, the respective distance $(\Delta\varphi$ in $\Sigma)$ between image elements has to be determined. Consequently the geometric assignment (φ, λ) for each image element of the appropriate reference track in the satellite system can be estimated by using Eq. (3).

Equation (4) is used for the transformation of coordinates (φ, λ) into geographical system Σ' with coordinates (φ', λ'). The third equation in (4) can be solved for φ'.

$$\varphi' = arcsin(sin\delta cos\varphi sin\lambda + cos\delta sin\varphi) \tag{10}$$

By using geographical longitude it has to be considered that the definition interval is given with $-180° < \lambda \leq 180°$. If a value or result of λ or λ' is outside this defined geographical interval, a back setting of this value will be executed by using Eq. (11):

$$\lambda_{red} = 2arctan(tan (\lambda/2)) \tag{11}$$

For the derivation of λ' the second equation in (4) is to divide by the first equation in (4).

$$(cos\varphi' sin\lambda')(cos\varphi' cos\lambda') = (cos\delta cos\varphi sin\lambda - sin\delta sin\varphi)/(cos\varphi cos\lambda) \tag{12}$$

After reducing and the introduction of the Tangency-function

$$tan \lambda' = cos \delta tan \lambda - sin \delta tan \varphi/ cos \lambda \tag{13}$$

Equation (12) can be solved for λ'.

$$\lambda' = arctan(cos \delta tan \lambda - sin \delta tan \varphi/ cos \lambda) \tag{14}$$

φ' and λ' are the coordinates of a satellite scene with an orbit defined in geographic coordinates $[\varphi' = 0, \lambda' = 0]$. After that, the image coordinates for the reference track in the geographical system Σ' with respect to the real coordinates in the rotating geographical system Σ'' has to be calculated. By rotation around the z-axis (North-South axis of Earth) with:

$$\Delta\lambda_0 = ABS(\lambda_{UL}^0 - \lambda_{UL}') \tag{15}$$

The reference image can be rotated in a way that the first line covers the first line in the original image, when placed in the system Σ'. λ_{UL}^0 is the longitude of the available geographical UL corner coordinate and λ_{UL}' is the corresponding longitude of UL after its inverse transformation from Σ (results of Eqs. (5) and (7)).

All additional lines of the two images which correspond to each other are moved because of the earth rotation. This additional shift caused by the earth rotation $\Delta\lambda_j^0$ of each single image line can be computed with the help of the differences in the length of the two left real geographic corner coordinates $(\lambda_{UL}^0, \lambda_{LL}^0)$ to the respective corresponding length $(\lambda_{UL}'^0, \lambda_{LL}^0)$ in the reference image:

$$\Delta\lambda_j^0 = j * ABS((\lambda_{UL}^0 - \lambda_{UL}'))/n; \quad n = \text{number of lines} \tag{16}$$

The calculation of λ_{LL}^0 is carried out accordingly to λ_{UL}^0, and by using $-\alpha/2$ in Eq. (7). The geographical latitude remains constant despite of earth rotation. The coordinates of the scene are completely available for all pixels after execution of the corrections of longitude λ':

$$\lambda_{i,j}'' = \lambda_{i,j}' + \Delta\lambda_0 + \Delta\lambda_j^0); \quad \text{for all } i,j \tag{17}$$

3.1.4   Pixel-Based Local Time Calculation

The next subtask calculates local time for each pixel of the scene. It can be shown (e.g. [22]) that for a satellite with a sun synchronous orbit the local crossing time (LCT) t_{LC} for the respective nadir point of the satellite orbit can be derived in dependence of its geographical latitude φ_N and a constant local equator crossing time (LECT) t_{LEC} based on the previously already known parameters.

$$t_{LC} = t_{LEC} - arcsin(tan\,\varphi_N cot\iota)/15; \quad \iota = \text{inclination of track} \tag{18}$$

The minus '−' in Eq. (18) refers to the descending node of the track. A precondition for Eq. (18) is the correct knowledge about calculation of t_{LEC}. Johnson et al. [22, p. 12] are referring that "ignoring any long-term drift, the time of a satellite pass measured in local solar time at nadir, is constant for given latitude." The time of a satellite pass includes the crossing of equator.

In [23, 24] Eq. (19) is used for determination of LECT ($t_{LEC} = t_{LC}$ for points with geographic latitude $\varphi = 0$) for mean solar conditions.

$$t_L = t_{LC} = t_{GM} + \lambda_G/15 \tag{19}$$

where: t_{GM} is the time of equator crossing in Greenwich Mean Time, GMT (in hours) [23] or in Coordinated Universal Time, UTC (in hours) [24]. But a well-known difference exists between Real and Mean Sun with the result that for instance local noon will change of −14 and +16 min within a year. This characteristic variation overlays the diurnal drift of equator crossing shown e.g. in [25] for NOAA-9 satellite.

By neglecting the orbit drift the time of equator crossing for Real Sun conditions will change in the same order within a year. This behaviour is caused by the elliptic orbit of Earth around sun and tilt of Earth's axis. This relation is described by the equation of time (t_E) which can be found e.g. in [26] and has to be considered as additional term on the right side of Eq. (19).

The Systems Tool Kit (STK) software [27] for orbit determination and the available two-line elements of LANDSAT-7 orbit were used to calculate t_{LEC} (in UTC) for each 21st day of the months for the year 2000. The simulated Real Sun t_{LEC} values (in hours) for the descending node are showing by asterisks in Fig. 3. Already with help of these 12 points is obvious, that the variation of t_{LEC} is similar to that of Equation of Time (t_E) [26]. Furthermore, if using Eq. (20) to determine t_{LEC} for Mean Sun a constant value was expected for LANDSAT satellite. But the difference between minimum and maximum of t_{LEC} for Mean Sun is around 2.5 min for the year 2000. The nearest t_{LEC} value to 10:06 a.m. (mean t_{LEC} of the 12 values) is given for 21st of June. If using the t_{LEC} and t_E for this date as basis (index 2106 in following equations), it is possible to describe the seasonal variation of t_{LEC} (in hours) in a first approximation with Eq. (20):

$$t_{LEC} = t_{LE2106} + (t_E + t_{E2106})/60; \quad (t_E, t_{E2106} \text{ in minutes}) \qquad (20)$$

The effect of orbital drift has to be included into Eq. (20) additionally. The inclusion of t_{LEC} of Eq. (20) into Eq. (18) results in Eq. (21).

$$t_{LC} = t_{LEC2106} + (t_E + t_{E2106})/60 - arcsin(tan\varphi_N cot\iota)/15 \qquad (21)$$

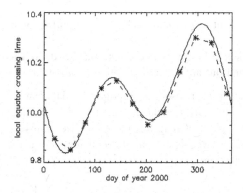

Fig. 3. Comparison of variation of t_{LEC} (in hours) for Real Sun determined for each 21st day of the month (year 2000 - dashed line) and simulated variation of t_{LEC} (in hours) determined by using Eq. (20) based on the defined reference point 21st June and equation of time computed for each day (year 2000 - solid line) for descending node of LANDSAT-7.

Equation (21) only applies to the nadir point of the satellite orbit. Therefore, the local time for all pixels of an image line have to be corrected by using their respective length difference $D\lambda'' = \lambda'' - \lambda_N''$ to the nadir point of this line by an additional term.

$$t_{LC} = t_{LEC2106} + (t_E + t_{E2106})/60 - arcsin(tan\varphi_N cot\imath)/15 + \Delta\lambda''/15 \qquad (22)$$

Thus, the geographical latitude and longitude as well as the corresponding local time for each pixel are available to calculate the solar zenith angle Θ_S. It depends on season and local time and can be calculated as

$$\Theta_S = arccos(sin\delta_S sin\varphi' + cos\delta_S cos\tau cos\varphi') \qquad (23)$$

where: φ' is the geographic latitude (Eq. 10), δ_S is the solar declination [26], and τ is the local time t_{LC} (Eq. 22) as angle.

3.1.5 Transformation of Topographic Information into Satellite Projection

Topographic information is an essential additional prerequisite for further automated processing (e.g. classification) of RS data. In cases of cloud-covered data it is useful to compare actual recorded data with a land-water mask to decide if clouds cover water or land e.g. in order to access the data usability for land applications.

As a rule for this, satellite data are corrected based on a topographical basis to make further processing of the data (e.g. atmospheric correction or thematic classification and value adding) possible. As a result of the transformation into the topographic projection the satellite image is larger, and consequently, triangles with no-data values on the four image borders will be generated (see Fig. 4b). This results in a decreasing performance of the processor.

Making very fast processing possible, the precursor procedure "Transformation of topographic Information into Satellite Projection" was developed and used here. The advantages are:

- A processor component is a structure analysis computing the connectivity of cloud pixels.
- A land-water mask is a binary image unlike the RS data. Therefore, a clear allocation can be carried out at the transformation of the data.

These considerations presupposed, the topographic data can be transformed into an image covering the satellite image data (hereafter referred as satellite projection[11]) as described in [28]. Each pixel of map has the same size as pixels of image. Figure 4 demonstrates schematically the operation steps for delivering the topographic information in satellite projection.

---

[11] The term Satellite Projection as it is used here is no projection in real sense of the word. A LANDSAT data track is resulting of sequential lines along the satellite path. Each line is a central projection from the satellite position.

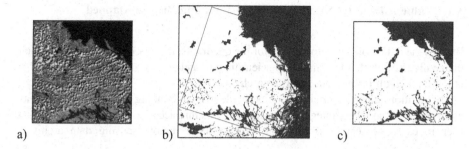

a)   b)   c)

Fig. 4. Topographic information in satellite projection (blue: water; white: land) (adopted and modified by [28] (a) LANDSAT data (Stockholm-region 2002/06/01) (RGB: band 7, 5, 3). (b) Map in Lambert projection with inscribed region of quick-look-data as given in (a). (c) Resulting land-water mask after transformation (b) on basis of coordinates (as additional layer of satellite data). (Color figure online)

3.2 Value Added Processing

3.2.1 Classification of Quick-Look-Data

The aim of a classification scheme is based on grouping objects with the same feature properties to pre-defined criteria and the differentiation to other objects which do not show these feature properties.

The available methods for classification are distinguished in supervised and unsupervised methods which can be applied interactively or automatically to a given data set. The used classification procedures in the data usability processor operate automatically on a pre-defined classification scheme. The used LANDSAT-7/ETM + -classification schemes are the NASA-ACCA (NASA - National Aeronautics and Space Administration) [15] and the ACRES-ACCA-procedure (National Earth Observation Group - previously known as ACRES) [16]. The NASA-procedure was developed as a component of the operative processing chain of the LANDSAT ground station at EROS Data Center in Sioux Falls [15], while the ACRES-procedure was integrated in the operative LANDSAT-processing chain of ACRES [16].

The potential to process JPEG-compressed quick-look-data of both established automatic cloud cover assessment (ACCA) procedures were analysed by [3]. The results of the classification can be seen as satisfactory for the application to JPEG-compressed quick-look-data and the processing time is minimal.

3.2.2 Structure Analysis of Classified Data

The procedure used for analysing cloud deviation structure within an assessment unit and for deriving indicators to estimate the usability of RS data is described by [13].

Direction filters [29, 30] are used for the determination of the cloud distribution in the scene, to estimate in the eight predefined directions the distance of undisturbed pixels. The eight matrices for both the cloud mask and cloud-free comparison mask are the result of filtering. The minimal distance value is determined by use of a minimum operator and stored into a temporary result matrix for both masks. The results of the structure analysis are handed over to the sub-module for assessing the data usability value.

3.3 Value Adding LANDSAT-7/ETM + Data and Browse Mapped Products

Besides the data usability information for the quadrants, the procedure delivers for each image diverse selected technical and scientific parameters as browsable products. This is the final result of the data processing chain.

In addition, other information can be made available taking different requirements and various processing strategies of optical RS data into account. The results support an user in cases of search for optimal data in large remote sensing data archives.

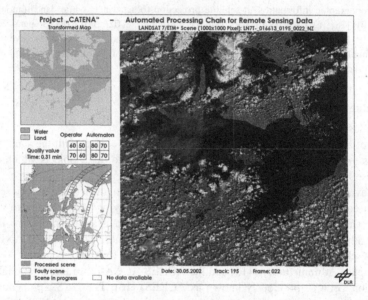

Fig. 5. Browse product to support interactive visual data quality assessment.

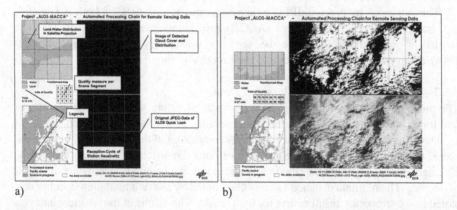

Fig. 6. Result of data usability assessment of ALOS data (adopted and modified by [28]) (a) browse product with annotation of its parts, (b) sample of an ALOS browse product.

Additionally, the information about the data quality (comparison of votes by operator and automat are included) can be used as matrix to control the processing/post-processing of RS data within an automatic process chain.

An example for a browsable product supporting an interactive visual data usability assessment by interpreters/operators is given in Fig. 5. The product includes the transformed topographic map given in satellite perspective (top left), the satellite orbit with track and frame (bottom left) and the quick-look with red rendered clouds (right).

4 Conclusions

The demand for area-wide (large area covering) environmental information permanently increases. The provision of this information, based on EO data, only can be guaranteed by automatic and operative processing. In principle, the method developed for automated quality assessment of LANDSAT data can be applied to other satellite data. In addition, the algorithms were already generalized by e.g. including a varying size of the images and by adoption satellite systems with a tilting sensor, here namely for the ALOS sensor system (Fig. 6). Figure 6a explains the individual elements included in the browsable product of changing size of data. Figure 6b shows a sample of a real ALOS browse product.

The continuously increasing number of RS missions, sensors and different data set available, as well as the considerably improved computer power and storage performance, including the ongoing improvement of automation of RS interpretation offer new possibilities in value adding of RS data for diverse applications. The requirements of the ESA on the functionality of the introduced processor have shown the following aspects:

1. Generic and automated RS data interpretation providing near real time data information products for time-critical applications is a service that has to be realised urgently.
2. Nevertheless that the respective interpretation processor provides only a selected set of information, a high-level of accuracy has to be guaranteed.
3. The developed processor includes all essential modules needed for processing of tailored products providing information for the user.
4. The basic structure of the presented processing chain was used to derive dynamic land-water masks (MERIS-, AATSR-, VEGETATION-data) in the ESA CCI project "Burned Area". A self-learning classification algorithm was developed for uncompressed data in order to derive the masks [31, 32].

Acknowledgement. The authors thank Dr. Berutti, Dr. Pitella, Dr. Biasutti (all European Space Agency) for the provided test data, for the constructive discussions, and the shown interest in our investigations. The authors wish to thanks E. Schwarz from the German Remote Date Center, Department of National Ground Segment Neustrelitz for his activities for determination of the actual equator crossing time.

References

1. EU. http://ec.europa.eu/enterprise/policies/space/gmes/. Accessed 06 Aug 2012
2. Borg, E., Fichtelmann, B., Asche, H.: Assessment for remote sensing data: accuracy of interactive data quality interpretation. In: Murgante, B., Gervasi, O., Iglesias, A., Taniar, D., Apduhan, B.O. (eds.) ICCSA 2011. LNCS, vol. 6783, pp. 366–375. Springer, Heidelberg (2011). doi:10.1007/978-3-642-21887-3_29
3. Borg, E., Fichtelmann, B., Asche, H.: Cloud classification in JPEG-compressed remote sensing data (LANDSAT 7/ETM +). In: Murgante, B., Gervasi, O., Misra, S., Nedjah, N., Rocha, A.M.A.C., Taniar, D., Apduhan, B.O. (eds.) ICCSA 2012. LNCS, vol. 7334, pp. 347–357. Springer, Heidelberg (2012). doi:10.1007/978-3-642-31075-1_26
4. Lau, W.-L., Li, Z.-L., Lam, K.W.-K.: Effects of JPEG compression on image classification. Int. J. Remote Sens. 24(7), 1535–1544 (2003)
5. Berutti, V.: LANDSAT 7 ESA Stations Network Report - Focus on Product Generation, LTWG 11, LANDSAT Technical Working Group Meeting (USGS/NASA), Canberra, Australia, 4–8 February, 21 p. (2002)
6. Bettac, H.-D., Reiniger, K., Brieß, K., Borg, E.: DLR/DFD presentation to the LGSOWG-30 Meeting, LGSOWG Meeting, Orlando, Florida, USA, 12–15 November, 22 p. (2001)
7. Pollex, J.: Oral communication (2011)
8. Schwarz, J., Bettac, H.D., Missling, K.-D.: Das DFD-Bodensegment für LANDSAT-7, DLR-Mitteilung 1999–2003, Mehl, D. (Eds.), Wessling, Germany, 20–21 October, pp. 49–56 (2000)
9. Biasutti, R., 2000, Cloud Cover Evaluation, LTWG 8, LANDSAT Technical Working Group Meeting (USGS/NASA), Ottawa, Canada, July 17–22, 10 p
10. Richter, R., Schläpfer, D.: Atmospheric/Topographic Correction for Satellite Imagery. DLR, Wessling (2011). DLR report DLR-IB 565-02/11
11. Huang, L., Li, Z.: Feature-based image registration using the shape context. Int. J. Remote Sens. 31(8), 2169–2177 (2010)
12. Borg, E., Fichtelmann, B., Böttcher, J., Günther, A., 2009, Processing of remote sensing data, EP 1 637 838 B1
13. Borg, E., Fichtelmann, B.: Verfahren und Vorrichtung zum Feststellen einer Nutzbarkeit von Fernerkundungsdaten, DP 10 2004 024 595 B3 (2004)
14. NASA 2011. http://landsathandbook.gsfc.nasa.gov/. Accessed 06 Aug 2012
15. Irish, R.: LANDSAT 7 Automatic Cloud Cover Assessment. In: Sylvia, D. (Eds.) Proceedings of SPIE (4049) Algorithms for Multispectral, Hyperspectral, and Ultraspectral Imagery VI, pp. 348–355 (2000)
16. Xu, Q., Wu, W.: ACRES Automatic Cloud Cover Assessment of LANDSAT 7 Images, Spatial Sciences Conference 2003 – Spatial Knowledge Without Boundaries Canberra, September 23–26, 10 p (2003)
17. Slater, P.N., Biggar, S.F., Holm, R.G., Jackson, R.D., Mao, Y., Moran, M.S., Palmer, J.M., Yuan, B.: Reflectance and radiance-based methods for the in-flight absolute calibration of multispectral sensors. Remote Sens. Environ. 22, 11–37 (1987)
18. Markham, B.L., Barker, J.L.: Spectral characterization of the LANDSAT thematic mapper sensors. Int. J. Remote Sens. 6, 697–716 (1985)
19. Chander, G., Markham, B.L., Helder, D.L.: Summary of current radiometric calibration coefficients for LANDSAT MSS, TM, ETM+, and EO-1 ALI sensors. Remote Sens. Environ. 113, 893–903 (2009). http://landportal.gsfc.nasa.gov/Documents/Landsat_Calibration_Summary.pdf. Accessed 20 Feb 2012

20. Gurney, R.J., Hall, D.K.: Satellite-derived surface energy balance estimates in the Alaskan Sub-Arctic. J. Clim. Appl. Meteorol. **22**(1), 115–125 (1983)
21. MATHEMATIK, Kleine Enzyklopädie, Verlag Enzyklopädie, Leipzig (1970)
22. Johnson, D.B., Flament, P., Bernstein, R.L.: High-resolution satellite imagery for mesoscale meteorological studies. Bull. Am. Meteorol. Soc. **75**, 5–34 (1994)
23. Wu, Z.-J., McAvaney, B.: Sampling methods for climate model calculated brightness temperatures. BMRC Research Report No. 117, Bureau of Meteorology, Australia (2005)
24. Ignatov, A., Lazlo, I., Harrod, E.D., Kidwell, K.B., Goodrum, G.P.: Equator crossing times for NOAA, ERS and EOS sun-synchronous satellites. Int. J. Remote Sens. **25**, 5255–5266 (2004)
25. Bush, K.A., Smith, G.L., Young, D.F.: The NOAA-9 earth radiation budget experiment wide field-of-view data set. In: 10th Conference on Atmospheric Radiation, June 1999, NASA 1999 Technical Docs (1999)
26. Duffett-Smith, P.: Practical Astronomy with Your Calculator, 3rd edn. Cambridge University Press, Port Melbourne, Cambridge, Madrid) (1988)
27. Analytical Graphics, Inc. http://www.agi.com/
28. Fichtelmann, B., Borg, E., Kriegel, M.: Verfahren zur operationellen Bereitstellung von Zusatzdaten für die automatische Fernerkundungsdatenverarbeitung, 23. In: Salzburg, S. et al. (Eds.) AGIT-Symposium, pp. 12–20. Wichmann, Berlin, Offenbach (2011)
29. Lehmann, T., Oberschelp, W., Pelikan, E., Repges, R.: Bildverarbeitung für die Medizin-Grundlagen Modelle, Methoden, Anwendungen, p. 462. Springer, Heidelberg (1997)
30. Haberäcker, P.: Praxis der digitalen Bildverarbeitung und Mustererkennung. Hanser, München (1995)
31. Fichtelmann, B., Borg, E.: A new self-learning algorithm for dynamic classification of water bodies. In: Murgante, B., Gervasi, O., Misra, S., Nedjah, N., Rocha, A.M.A.C., Taniar, D., Apduhan, B.O. (eds.) ICCSA 2012. LNCS, vol. 7335, pp. 457–470. Springer, Heidelberg (2012). doi:10.1007/978-3-642-31137-6_35
32. Fichtelmann, B., Guenther, K.P., Borg, E.: Adaption of a self-learning algorithm for dynamic classification of water bodies to SPOT VEGETATION Data. In: Gervasi, O., Murgante, B., Misra, S., Gavrilova, M.L., Rocha, A.M.A.C., Torre, C., Taniar, D., Apduhan, B.O. (eds.) ICCSA 2015. LNCS, vol. 9158, pp. 177–192. Springer, Heidelberg (2015). doi:10.1007/978-3-319-21410-8_14

Automated Spatial Data Processing and Refining

Marion Simon[✉] and Hartmut Asche

Geoinformation Research Group, Department of Geography,
University of Potsdam, Potsdam, Germany
{marion.simon,hartmut.asche}@uni-potsdam.de

Abstract. This paper focuses on the definition of a method for data processing by means of automated professional map generation. For this, initially services have to be identified that represents cartographic rules and recommendations. In order to link those services with respect to their cartographic content and to control the process within a component, a set of rules has to be designed. This is explained by examples and can be used as a template pattern for other services. Individual services and modules within the process will be arranged hierarchically on the basis of the cartographic visualisation pipeline. Its consequent graphical classification is presented. The aim is to prepare the theoretical cartographic basis in a formal way, which should enable technical implementation without cartographic technical expertise.

Keywords: Geovisualisation · Rule-based map construction · Mapping assistant service · Cartographic visualisation pipeline · Cartographic services

1 Introduction

Since 1972, when the first operational remote sensing satellite provided digital data of our environment, the amount of geospatial data has been increasing at an exponential rate. To process and analyse such geodata, dedicated ICT systems (information and communication technology) systems called geographic information or, in short, geoinformation systems (GIS) have been developed. Geodata modelling and analysis can be considered their prominent strength, visualisation in cartographic modelling quality their major weakness. In contrast, graphic-oriented map design systems provide extensive drawing and design functions but lack non-graphic data management and analysis capabilities. Recent years have seen a constantly growing demand for maps combining cartographic visualisation for visual analysis and interaction with the underlying geodata for non-graphic data manipulation and analysis. At the same time, map production and geodata processing technologies employed by commercial map producers do not facilitate an integrated production process for the generation of maps in cartographic modelling quality from geospatial databases. This situation poses a major economic problem which has caused a significant number of map producers to cease operations in the last decade. The research presented here addresses this problem. It aims at developing a technology concept allowing for the integrated processing and construction of non-graphic and graphic cartographic products from existing geodata.

© Springer International Publishing AG 2016
A.-L. Lamprecht (Ed.): ISoLA 2012/2014, CCIS 683, pp. 38–49, 2016.
DOI: 10.1007/978-3-319-51641-7_3

The key objective is to design and implement a modular, scalable workflow that processes geospatial input data into application-specific quality geodata and map products. It is obvious that professional and economic expertise of a commercial map producer is essential for the success of the research.

In the past decades, extensive research has been carried out on GIS, geodata acquisition and filtering, geodatabases and geodata management as well as on digital map construction and geovisualisation [1, 2]. Map production processes from geodata stocks have received much less attention [3]. Projects relevant to the research dealt with here include the development of a now operational process for the automated construction of quality map graphics [4] and the ongoing development of a map construction assistant facilitating a rule-based map construction process for cartographic visualisation of statistical mass data [5]. These projects and other related research work provide an appropriate basis for our research. Combining available geodata processing and map production functions in one process will, however, not bridge the gap between professional geodata modelling and professional map construction. What is required is an integrated, software-driven process in which dedicated data and map modelling modules interact to produce application-specific geodata sets or cartographic maps or interactive data-based geovisualisations.

The contribution of this paper is presenting a method for building up a rule-based modularised process for automated quality map construction that can be implemented as a mapping assistant service. The next section of this paper describes the overall approach in the field of developing a process for automated map construction. Section 3 focuses on the characteristics of one selected map representation type as an example for showing developed method of process definition. Finally, in Sect. 4, some conclusions and open questions are discussed.

2   Materials and Methods

A process for automated data processing is the focus of several professional disciplines. Automated map production researchers are dealing with this issue since decades without having arrived at a conclusive solution yet. In this work the perspective comes from geoinformatics and deals with a method for automated map construction. Building on the classical visualisation pipeline [6], general working steps in map production are integrated [5, 7]. For automation within a service those modules are split up in submodules based on identified rules, definitions and recommendations from literature. Therefore a collection of rules in natural language is built up and classified to matching module components. A visualisation of relations and dependencies between modules is done with jABC (Java Application Building Center) framework [8]. The visualisation of graphs precedes a development of a typology for subsequently creation of fomalised rule-sets. This paper shines a light on the visualisation process in general (Fig. 1) and how it could be used for developing a process chain for automated map production. Additionally a rule set for setting case sensitive sequential process definitions will be discovered. Both could be used for developing a so called Mapping Assistant Service.

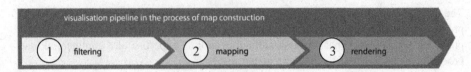

Fig. 1. Visualisation pipeline in the process of map construction by Mapping Assistant Service [5]

In this work the model of the visualisation pipeline provides the base for embedding additional sub-processes. The visualisation pipeline for automated professional map generation consists of the core processes filtering, mapping and rendering at the upper hierarchical level. These core processes are first explained below in general and then partly broken down to the necessities of a Mapping Assistant Service.

For the prototype, the presented sequence is used as a basis for embedding sub-processes and services which are presented as sub-models in different hierarchical levels.

Filtering means data processing which can be carried outfor example by completing, reducing or filtering the amount of raw data. This core process includes acquisition or editing metadata equally. The following step of mapping comprises mapping of the pre-processed geometry data including their attributes. Transformation of presented data into image data and/or into a digital image is called rendering. Following Kucharczyk [7], the three featured core processes are partly further split by means of map production.

2.1 Filtering Module

Correction of erroneous values and changes in the data basis as well as calculation of new values out of the existing should be provided by the service (Fig. 2).

Fig. 2. Cartographic processes within filtering module

These functionalities increase output quality on the one hand. On the other hand a representation of relations between data could generate new knowledge to the user. Basically, an error-free and complete data set should be available for use. Since the mapping assistant service is a software for representation of statistical mass data with its spatial reference, it should be possible to calculate statistical characteristics (stored as new values). In the preparation process of statistical information, the correlation and regression analysis, determination of frequency distributions, standard deviations and confidence intervals is recommended by Hake et al. [9].

Scale-dependent options are possible in further process flow. An output map scale (target scale) could be fixed at the very first beginning setup of using the assistant, but after this point within the process it has to be specified by the user. Since the output parameters (e.g. layout design, map-scale, medium, title of map) could in theory also be queried at this point by the user, this process step has not been taken from the graph. Kucharczyk [7] distinguishes between determining spatial reference and allocation of projection. Here, a georeferencing module comprises both mentioned sub-processes. It includes checking spatial extent (geographical bounding box defined by north-, south-, east-, west-limitation), geocoding or transformation of geodata as well as choosing and application of optimal projection. An automated selection of an appropriate carto-graphic representation method necessitates a preceding data analysis module for examining present meta data. The analysis covers geodata on dimension (D), semantic information (S), scaling niveau (SN), attribute value (A), attribute value course (AV) and time relation (T). Model generalisation is according to Schürer [10] the transformation of an object model "with respect to its semantic and/or geometric res-olution, its data model and its structure simplified or in a new digital object model".

2.2 Mapping Module

To proceed with the selection of a cartographic representation method the system gets the outcomes of the data analysis. Within the step of object sign referencing, it comes to the linking of symbols and geo-objects. Finally the process step map sign con-struction complements the mapping part. This predetermined sequence is used to design an entry for the prototype. Because of the differentiation of the last two steps it can be assumed that either the appropriate cartographic symbol for a geo object does not exist, or that the user is free to generate symbols. A module for map symbol construction ensures a gap closure and requires a return loop for object sign referencing for assignment of the new cartographic symbol to related spatial data.

A renouncement of mentioned map symbol construction modules for prototype development is feasible (Fig. 3). For the prototype, development should be dispensed with map symbol construction first. Instead, the symbol library should have sufficient symbols for topographic base maps as well as thematic content representation in stock.

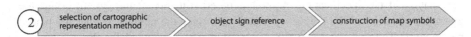

Fig. 3. Cartographic processes within mapping module

2.3 Rendering Module

The third core process of the visualization pipeline (Fig. 4) begins with the represen-tation of referenced map symbols. Thereafter cartographic generalisation for visual optimisation of a cartographic representation follows. The map production in carto-graphic quality depends on this sub-process. It contains "necessary respectively applicable processes and types of generalisation and abstraction that leads to a transfer of differentiated and detailed reality into an expressive map representation" [11]. Objective (e.g. map border, map field, map frame) and semantic map components (e.g. map content, map title, map grid) all together make up the marginal data. The map composition includes the creative round off to finalise the cartographic result and should be, according to Kucharczyk [7], partially left to the user. For this last process step within the visualisation pipeline, an editor is conceivable, which includes components for printing, exporting or saving the map product.

Fig. 4. Cartographic processes within rendering module

3 Mapping Assistant Service

A process has been conceptualised starting from customer-centred geodata input to enterprise-based data filtering, analysis of visualisation options communicated to and endorsed by the customer, automated map or geodata generation according to the specifications agreed on, prototype production, again communicated to and approved by the customer, to the customised final product and delivery to the customer.

For implementation of cartographic representation methods within a mapping assistant service their specific characteristics must be identified. It contains features of spatial data as well as design elements and its possible variations depending on data basis.

3.1 Set of Rules

A modularised implementation of the components should be considered in the context of a rule-based system. According to Uthe [12] a rule-based system consists "of a database with valid facts, the rules for the derivation of new facts in the knowledge base and the rule interpreter for controlling the efficient selection and execution of rules that perform certain actions". A set of rules is based on the defined requirement formulation of the specification. A module-based structure of the system brings the guarantee of clarity of the regulatory framework, since the number of rules are placed per module. The importance of rules is exemplarily constituted for the sub-process (second hierarchical level of visualisation pipeline) selection of cartographic representation method, its design elements and the variations thereof. For the development of the regulations, a typology is always created, which can be applied in their scheme to other sub-processes or modules.

The presented rule set uses results generated in the filtering-module *data analysis* and stored as variables D, S, SN, A, AV and T (see Chap. 2.1). For building up a rule set structure a method of Germany's Federal Ministry of Transport and Digital Infrastructure (BMVBS) [13] served as a basis. Following BMVBS the "elements of a rule-based system are existing rules composed of a condition part (premise) and an action part (conclusion)" [13]. From the cartographic point of view.

1. Selection of an optimal cartographic representation method (phase 1),
2. Linking of design elements and cartographic representation methods (phase 2),
3. Linking of variations and design elements (phase 3).

Selection of Cartographic Representation Method. Phase 1 involves the selection of the optimal cartographic representation method (here: RM) for given data to be visualised. The available methods are summarised in the corresponding typology (Fig. 5). Based on the analysis results from the data pre-processing (data analysis), the selection-default is embedded in the set of rules and the results are stored for further processing, in the cache, for example, in a variable RM.

level 1			level 2		
code	abb. design.	designation	code	abb. design.	designation
M1	RM	cartographic representation method	M11	RM_MDS	method of diagram signatures
			M12	RM_MDM	method of diagram maps
			M13	RM_MPS	method of positionsignatures
			M14	RM_CMG	method of choropleth mapping related to geometric referenced area

Fig. 5. Typology of cartographic representation methods (RM)

The set of rules to be implemented rests upon the results of the requirements analysis for a prototype of the assistant as well as on representation methods identified as necessary based on the component data analysis within the filtering process, in order to reflect any kind of data basis. In order to meet the above condition, the results of data analysis (data preparation) have to be read out in a first step by the system and to be complied with the subsequent election of the representation method in Fig. 6 listed specifications.

Linking of Design Elements. Phase 2 specifies the representation of the selected method by assigning the design element(s) (area, diagram, signature line and line with arrow), which are treated as separate modules in the system. The result of this phase is for further system access, here in the variable DE (design element) cached. The assigned notational conventions define the appearance of visualisation in principle without defining the unique appearance. This separation of design elements and variables is used for the sake of clarity with respect to the portion of dependencies modules to each other. From a business perspective the assignation of design elements as realisation of specifications is necessary, whereby said module parts are inferior to the hierarchical level of the module design element.

Linking of Variables. In Phase 3 the linking of design elements and the modules for the variation takes place. Variations (size, shape, direction, colour, brightness and pattern) can be limited for certain design elements. A basic allocation of variations to

code	cartographic representation method (phase 1)	specification (related to data basis)	premise
1	RM_MDS	selection for data with point-dimension in combination with quantitative semantic information	D = „point" AND S = „quantitative"
2	RM_MDM	selection for data with area-dimension in combination with quantitative semantic information	D = „area" AND S = „quantitative"
3	RM_MPS	selection for data with point-dimension in combination with qualitative semantic information	D = „point" AND S = „qualitative"
4	RM_CMG	~tion for data with areal-~ombina~	~ = „area" AND

Fig. 6. Rule set – Selection of optimal cartographic representation method (RM)

design elements is excluded due to professional dependencies. A variation in the brightness is at least in the design element signature applicable, if the scale is ordinal and the RM method of position signatures is used. Accordingly, it is at this point necessary for the system, as in the selection of cartographic representation method, to again access the results from the data analysis.

3.2   Process Definition by Example

This use case aims at an automated cartographic production of an economic map by assistant. The chosen digital dataset contains feature classes relating economic data of Germany in the year 2006 [14]. The amount of working population, differed by economic sector, describes the economic structure for each administrative district (NUTS 2-level). For orientation, further topological data (e.g. river, administrative borders, capital cities of federal states) are contained. This use case focuses on processing data to thematic map representation under consideration of given and processed topological data representation.

Based on the described dataset process, steps of the filtering module can mostly be skipped. There is no need for correction of erroneous values or calculation of new values. Map scale depends (in this case) on spatial extent and size of output medium. For this use case a map scale 1:2,500,000 is calculated and suggested to the user by the assistant automatically. The georeferencing sub-module is skipped as well. The given dataset contains spatial metadata for projection. These metadata will be compared with default reference coordinate systems held by the service. Loaded data will be checked for delivered coordinate systems and projection parameters by the Mapping Assistant Service. A data analysis will be done automatically. It determines topological spatial structure, data dimension and semantic information. Depending on the outcome further data attributes were determined. For this case an extended analysis is not necessary. This analysis module cooperates with the mapping module selection of cartographic representation method (RM). This prevents calculations that are not needed for dedicating the optimal RM. Furthermore the data analysis tool determines the need for data classification. In this use case the mapping assistant service will initiate a classification within the following module *model generalisation*. This is necessary for the cartographic generalisation module within the rendering sub-process, described below.

The selection of the cartographic representation method realises the first step in the mapping part of the visualisation pipeline. It uses the outcomes of the data analysis-module to modify the production process for this certain case. Asche et al. [15] describe the complex selection process for an appropriate cartographic representation for each possible combination of data characteristics method by UML (Unified Modeling Language). Going through the mentioned process the following outcome will appear for this example of an economic map of Germany 2006: The topological spatial structure is discrete. The amount of working population is given by the year 2006. There is no continuous value representation. Data dimension is area, because the values are related to an administrative unit. The amounts of working population are data with quantitative semantic information. This leads as seen in Fig. 7, to the choice of method of diagram maps (RM_MDM).

An object sign reference module contains the rules for a connection of data to libraries containing design elements and related variations. In our sample case, the design element *diagram* is allowed for representing the given data. The user can choose the diagram style (circle, bar, square chart). For this paper diagram style circular chart is chosen by the user. A variation of this chosen design element size and colour is allowed. For a monochrome representation grey is chosen. The user is also allowed to define if the size of the circular chart should also represent the total amount of working population. A static size only represent the portions of economic sectors.

The basemap must be brighter than the represented theme to guarantee the semantic hierarchy and the readability of the map. Depending on brightness, saturation and colour of a basemap, the assistant offers through rules the only possible range of grey variation to the user. A module for construction of map symbols will be passed by, because standard options are sufficient to represent the amount of working population of Germany in 2006 related to federal states. Size of diagram style circle is proven by the system. Sizes are oriented to smallest and biggest administrative area and amount of working population (in case of dynamic diagram size) and are not allowed to contact or overlap borders of related areas.

A graphical output like Fig. 8 on the whole dataset is first given in the first module of the rendering process. The application of map symbols is done, so visual impression of the potential map is possible. Conflicts in graphical output can be analysed. For correction of cartographic conflicts the following module is implemented. Cartographic generalisation is one of the most important modules in high quality map production process. One problem of a representation of single quantitative data related to administrative borders by diagram could be on side of theme: position and size of diagram-circles (overlaying boundaries) as well as minimum distances that makes modification necessary. On side of basemap simplification of boundaries (terrestrial as

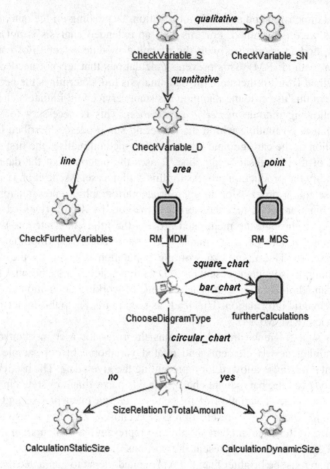

Fig. 7. Implemented process for RM selection in jABC

well as land-ocean-borders) could be necessary. Overall goal of cartographic gener-alisation is to maximise expressivity, effectivity and adequacy.

Sub-processes, as a result of splitting a complex process, and their further sub-processes are interrelated. A graphical representation of these divided connections leads to a hierarchical structure. Before process elements will be implemented by algorithms, this division into sub-processes will be continued down to service level. After structuring of logical relationships activity diagrams can arise, that can be shown by means of UML notation. Sub-processes of the rendering were used exemplarily to demonstrate the embedding of nested processes in its various hierarchical levels. The amount of hierarchical levels is not fixed. Within the rendering four hierarchies resulted (not sure what this means). The detailed design of the map construction process by means of a map construction assistant is now initiated. The technical interpretation clarifies the hierarchical construction of the services. A cartographic interpretation will not be stated in this paper.

Fig. 8. Output of process on given dataset on economic structure of Germany 2006, subdivided into five sectors in relation to working population (excerpt, not scaled)

4   Conclusion

The technological concept outlined in this paper is, to our knowledge, novel in the following aspects. First, it integrates the customer into the process via an internet-based portal enabling her to influence the generation of the end product within the scope of professional geodata processing and visualisation principles implemented in the respective modules. Second, a double-track process will be developed to generate either or both graphic or non-graphic geodata products. Due to the software limitations mentioned in chapter 1, such process is not operational in commercial production environments. Third, an automatic data-to-map transformation procedure will be provided. Such rule-based transformation of a filtered geodata model into a corresponding map model by data-to-localised-symbol mapping and generalisation procedures is rarely implemented in commercial map production. Fourth, development and implementation of the production process will be based on software components, such as the jABC (Java Application Building Center) framework. At present, the majority of geodata production processes is based on commercial software products with the strengths and weaknesses outlined above.

In the early stages of our research, a generic map construction process based on the jABC framework was developed. This needs to be elaborated and extended to cover the complete geodata and map generation process. On a conceptual level, the geospatial data processing and map generation processes will have to be broken down into elementary sub-processes to finally allow for a greater degree of scalability and automation. This will be complemented by an examination of potential system environments. The resulting preliminary process defined and implemented on a working basis will then be evaluated for its functionality and economic viability with real-world sample data from the collaborating cartographic enterprise. Further development will be based on a mix of methods of which software engineering methods, rule-based map construction and geovisualisation principles are the most important.

Acknowledgement. The authors gratefully acknowledge the contribution of the following persons: Andrew Whelan (University of Limerick) for checking and correcting the English text of non-native speakers, Mirko Seifert (Universiy of Potsdam) for his help with the illustrations, and Anna-Lena Lamprecht (University of Limerick) for her patience and helpful advice on organising and writing this article. Thank you all.

References

1. Hardy, P.: High-quality cartography in a commodity GIS: experiences in development and deployment. In: ICA Symposium on Cartography for Central and Eastern Europe [CD-ROM], 16–17 February. Technische Universität Wien/International Cartographic Association, Wien (2009)
2. Buckley, A., Frye, C., Buttenfield, B.: An information model for maps: towards cartographic production from GIS databases. In: Proceedings of the 22nd International Cartographic Conference A Coruna (ICC 2005), Mapping Approaches into a Changing World, [CD-ROM], 9–16 July. International Cartographic Association, A Coruna (2005)
3. Engemaier, R., Asche, H.: CartoService: a web service framework for quality on-demand geovisualisation. In: Murgante, B., Gervasi, O., Iglesias, A., Taniar, D., Apduhan, Bernady, O. (eds.) ICCSA 2011. LNCS, vol. 6782, pp. 329–341. Springer, Heidelberg (2011). doi:10. 1007/978-3-642-21928-3_23
4. Asche, H., Stankute, S., Mueller, M., Pietruska, F.: Towards developing an integrated quality map production environment in commercial cartography. In: Murgante, B., Misra, S., Carlini, M., Torre, C.M., Nguyen, H.-Q., Taniar, D., Apduhan, B.O., Gervasi, O. (eds.) ICCSA 2013. LNCS, vol. 7974, pp. 221–237. Springer, Heidelberg (2013). doi:10.1007/ 978-3-642-39649-6_16
5. Simon, M.: Automatisierte Konstruktion thematischer Karten. Kartentypen, Prozessdefinition und Prozesssteuerung. Unpubl. Master thesis, University of Potsdam, Potsdam, pp. 2–24 (2014)
6. Haber, R.B., McNabb, D.A.: Visualization idioms: a conceptual model for scientific visualisation systems. In: Shriver, B., Nielsen, G.M., Rosenblum, M. (eds.) Visualization in Scientific Computing, pp. 74–93. IEEE Computer Society Press, Los Alamitos (1990)

7. Kucharczyk, C.: Konzeption, Entwicklung und Implementierung eines regelbasierten Kartenkonstruktionsassistenten zur fachgerechten Visualisierung statistischer Massendaten. Unpubl. Master thesis, University of Potsdam, Potsdam. pp. 80, 89, 96 (2013)

8. Steffen, B., Margaria, T., Nagel, R., Jörges, S., Kubczak, C.: Model-driven development with the jABC. In: Bin, E., Ziv, A., Ur, S. (eds.) HVC 2006. LNCS, vol. 4383, pp. 92–108. Springer, Heidelberg (2007). doi:10.1007/978-3-540-70889-6_7

9. Hake, G., Grünreich, D., Meng, L.: Kartographie: Visualisierung raum-zeitlicher Informationen. 8., vollst. neu bearb. u. erw. Aufl. Walter de Gruyter & Co., Berlin (2002)

10. Schürer, D.: Modellgeneralisierung, p. 30, 10:17 (2002). http://www.geoinformation.net/lernmodule/lm10/download/vgl_le5.pdf. Accessed 30 Sept 2015

11. Ogrissek, R. (ed.): abc Kartenkunde. 1. Aufl., p. 170. VEB F. A. Brockhaus Verlag, Leipzig (1983)

12. Uthe, A.-D.: Stichwort "regelbasiertes System". In: Bollmann, J., Koch, W.G. (eds.) Lexikon der Kartographie und Geomatik. A bis Z. CD-ROM. Spektrum Akademischer Verlag GmbH, Heidelberg, Berlin (2002)

13. BMVBS Bundesministerium für Verkehr, Bau und Stadtentwicklung; BBR Bundesamt für Bauwesen und Raumordnung (eds.) Automatische Ableitung von stadtstrukturellen Grundlagen und Integration in einem Geographischen Informationssystem, p. 21. Abschlussbericht. Schriftenreihe: Forschungen. Heft 134, Bonn (2008)

14. Breyer, J. (ed.): Haack Weltatlas. GIS-Unterricht mit Atlas und ArcGIS von ESRI. Buch mit CD-ROM, p. 32. Klett Verlag (2010)

15. Asche, H., Kucharczyk, C., Simon, M.: Geodata discovery assistant: a software module for rule-based cartographic visualisation and analysis of statistical mass data. In: Gervasi, O., Murgante, B., Misra, S., Gavrilova, M.L., Rocha, A.M.A.C., Torre, C., Taniar, D., Apduhan, B.O. (eds.) ICCSA 2015. LNCS, vol. 9157, pp. 566–575. Springer, Heidelberg (2015). doi:10.1007/978-3-319-21470-2_41

Automata Learning in Practice

Learning-Based Cross-Platform Conformance Testing

Johannes Neubauer[(✉)] and Bernhard Steffen

Technische Universität Dortmund, Dortmund, Germany
{johannes.neubauer,steffen}@cs.tu-dortmund.de

Abstract. In this paper we present learning-based cross-platform conformance testing (LCCT), an approach specifically designed to validate successful system migration. Key to our approach is the combination of (1) adequate user-level system abstraction, (2) higher-order integration of executable test-blocks, and (3) learning-based automatic model inference and comparison. The impact of LCCT will be illustrated along the migration of Springer's Online Conference Service (OCS) from a browser-based implementation to using a RESTful web service API. Continuous LCCT allowed us in particular to systematically pinpoint spots where the original OCS depended on browser-based access control mechanisms, to eliminate them, and thus to maintain the OCS access control policy for the RESTful API.

Keywords: Higher-order test-block integration · Automata learning conformance testing · User-level modeling

1 Motivation

More and more computer-aided processes move to the web. This is true for those that have its origin in manual processes in the real world like planning a scientific conference, but also for processes that have emerged with the web like social networks. The corresponding solutions – often subsumed by the notion *enterprise applications* – offer a web interface to the clients, so that they can interact with it like with a desktop application. Since the ecosystem in the internet is growing and there is a need for interaction between these different systems, there is a rapidly accumulating amount of services in the web offering an interface to other services, e.g., via web services [61] or RESTful services [12]. This trend results in increasingly complex systems, which have to be available 24/7, serve a high amount of users, and depend on other systems. From the point-of-view of a service provider this typically results in the pressure to rapidly adapt his systems without hampering its functionality as well as properties like security, availability, and consistency.

Ensuring these properties is a challenge for state-of-the-art testing approaches, since low-level tests cannot make proper propositions on higher levels of abstraction in particular over the user-level behavior of a complex system.

© Springer International Publishing AG 2016
A.-L. Lamprecht (Ed.): ISoLA 2012/2014, CCIS 683, pp. 53–79, 2016.
DOI: 10.1007/978-3-319-51641-7_4

Model-based testing [59] needs an a priori system specification, which is hard to provide and even harder to keep up-to-date with changes. This is the major hurdle for model-based testing to enter industrial practice. In contrast, test-based model extrapolation – better known as active automata learning [4,18] – enables to infer behavioral models of black-box systems without the need for such a specification. The manual effort boils down to implementing executable test blocks, which are then automatically combined to test runs. Learning technology then aggregates the information gained through test executions into behavioral models.

In this paper we present an approach to cross-platform conformance testing using automata-learning which is tailored to validate behavioral equivalence of different implementations of a given application. We focus here on platform changes, i.e., changes that should **not** change the behavior of a system. Such changes may be due to adaptions or technological switches in terms of operation system, programming language (e.g. reimplementation of legacy software), execution environment (e.g. application server), third-party components (e.g. database vendor, relational versus noSQL databases, or access-layer to the data-base), optimizations (e.g. caching or clustering), new access methods to the application (e.g. a RESTful API), or API changes of third-party services (like Facebook, Twitter, or Google Maps).

Essential for our learning-based approach to effectively work in practice are (cf. [62]):

Stable abstraction: System evolution and in particular platform migrations do not mean that the implementation changes arbitrarily. Rather, evolution of systems in wider use should support some form of downwards compatibility, in order to allow people to continue to work in the way they are used to. This does not mean that the underlying code is not changed/refactored, but this should not affect the way the user interacts with the system. Thus we base our approach on abstractions on the user-level which are meant to remain stable during platform migration.

Bridging implementation: The comfort of a common abstraction-level for all versions has to be supported technically by a mechanism that automatically takes care of providing the *test driver* (see Sect. 2.2) with the correct implementation.

We satisfy these needs by adopting

1. adequate user-level system abstraction,
2. higher-order test-block integration [39], as well as
3. learning-based automatic model inference and comparison.

The impact of LCCT will be illustrated along testing behavioral conformance of presentation and business logic layer of Springer's Online Conference Service (OCS), a complex business application. Indeed, behavioral equivalence between these layers has been a critical issue during a major refactoring process that enhanced the browser-based OCS with a RESTful web service API, in order to open its services to be used by other services in the web. The OCS is an online manuscript submission and review system and therefore offers crucial information to other services, like the list of authors of accepted papers in a conference, which may be used by a conference registration system. This way it is possible to track whether at least one author per accepted paper has registered and paid the conference fee in order to prevent authors not to show up on conference. In addition this is a good example for platform migrations that are an ongoing effort: the web interface is in use and advances further on. Accordingly, the RESTful API has to be adapted. Hence behavioral equivalence has to be tested continuously, too.

The paper is structured as follows. After describing our modeling framework, active automata learning, related work, and the web application we used in our experiments in Sect. 2, Sect. 3 describes the scenario for the case study of this paper, whereas Sect. 4 introduces LCCT. In Sect. 5 we show how we deployed LCCT to the Online Conference Service. Finally, Sect. 6 summarizes the results and outlines some future perspectives.

2   Preliminaries

In this section we present the *Java Application Building Center* (*jABC*) framework, which we enhance in this paper, as well as active automata learning, a discussion of related approaches like model-based testing and conformance testing, and the web application OCS, which serves as *System Under Learning* (*SUL*) during this paper.

2.1   Extreme Model-Driven Design in the jABC

The aforementioned user-level test blocks are realized in the jABC [27], a framework for service-oriented development that allows users to create services and applications easily by composing reusable building blocks into (flow-) graph structures that are both formally well-defined as well as easy to read and build. These building blocks are called *Service Independent building Blocks* (*SIBs*) in analogy to the telecommunication terminology [54], in the spirit of the service-oriented computing paradigm [24] and of the *One Thing Approach* [28], an evolution of the model-based lightweight coordination approach of [26] specifically applied to services.

The jABC follows the *eXtreme Model-Driven Design* (*XMDD*) of [31]. XMDD combines ideas from service orientation, model driven design and *eXtreme programming* (XP) and enables application experts to control the design and evolution of applications during their whole life-cycle on the basis of *Lightweight Process Coordination* (LPC) [26]. The SIBs are parameterizable, so that their behavior can be adapted depending on the current context of use. Furthermore, each SIB has one or more outgoing branches specifying its successor. Which branch of the SIB is used is determined at runtime.

On the basis of a large library of SIBs, the user builds models for the desired system in terms of hierarchical *Service Logic Graphs* [55] (*SLG*). SLGs are semantically interpreted (e.g., by a model checker) as *Kripke Transition Systems* (*KTS*), a generalization of both *Kripke Structures* (*KS*) and *Labeled Transition Systems* [33] (*LTS*) that allows labels both on nodes and edges. A KTS[1] over a finite set of atomic propositions AP is a structure $M = (S, Act, T, I)$, where

- S is a finite set of *states*.
- Act is a finite set of *actions*.
- $T \subseteq S \times Act \times S$ is a total *transition relation*.
- $I : S \to 2^{AP}$ is an *interpretation function*.

Nodes (SIBs) in the SLG are the activities and represent services, or an SLG as sub process in order to introduce hierarchy. The edges directly correspond to SIB branches: they describe how to continue the execution depending on the result of the previous activity. SIBs communicate via a shared resources concept. Its incarnation is called *execution context*, often abbreviated simply as *context*, which is itself hierarchical and addresses data objects via identifiers.

The service integration into the graphical process model design framework jABC is realized via an adapter pattern [56] (see Fig. 1) that supports domain-specific (business) activities [11]. A service is integrated by a technical expert, who implements two artifacts:

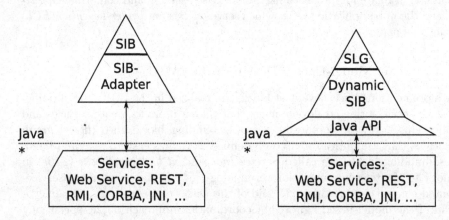

Fig. 1. The original SIB adapter pattern of the jABC.

Fig. 2. The new dynamic SIB pattern of the jABC.

1. a service independent building block (SIB) in form of a Java class defining the parameters, documentation, and appearance of the activity and

---

[1] A KS is a KTS with an empty set of actions, an LTS is a KTS with a trivial interpretation I.

2. a *SIB adapter* in form of a static method written in the corresponding target language for processing the parameters. The adapter calls the service, and evaluates the result in order to find the successor activity.

Being organized in taxonomies, these activities can easily be discovered and (re)used for building complex process models, the aforementioned service logic graphs, in the corresponding graphical development environment, the jABC. The adapter pattern allows for arbitrary domain-specific activities which interact via their common *context* of resources. In this paper we will introduce the refinement to the new dynamic SIB pattern (see Fig. 2).

2.2   Active Automata Learning

Test-based model extrapolation (active automata learning), in particular the algorithm L^* [4], has been developed to infer deterministic finite state acceptors. In practical settings, this approach may be interpreted as a systematic test generation framework that interrogates the *system under learning (SUL)* and infers an appropriate model. In real world situations SULs often behave like reactive systems, e.g., a web-service or in the case of the OCS as a complete web application. *Mealy machines* are an adequate automata formalism to express deterministic input-output behavior recorded from the test cases conducted from a learning algorithm. To extrapolate system behavior from reactive systems, Angluin's algorithm has been generalized to L_M^* in order to work for Mealy machines [25].

A Mealy machine is a tuple $M = (Q, q_0, \Sigma, \Gamma, \delta, \gamma)$ where

- Q is a finite nonempty set of *states*,
- $q_0 \in Q$ is the *initial state*,
- Σ is a finite *input alphabet*,
- Γ is a finite *output alphabet*,
- $\delta : Q \times \Sigma \to Q$ is the *transition function*, and
- $\gamma : Q \times \Sigma \to \Gamma$ is the *output function*.

A learning algorithm poses *membership queries (MQ)* in the form of a sequence of *input symbols* $w_i \in \Sigma^*$ called *input word* and receives a sequence of *output symbols* $w_o \in \Gamma^*$ called *output word*. The former have to be mapped to calls on the SUL and the answers of the system have to be translated back to output symbols. This is done by a *test driver*, which executes the test sequences on the system and interprets the results into two or more output categories (the formerly mentioned output symbols), which resembles a lot to classical testing approaches. In testing, we typically have either the outcome **pass** or **fail**. These may be represented by corresponding outputs in a Mealy machine.

The used algorithm proceeds by iterating two phases, namely test-based modeling and model-based testing. The phases are alternatingly repeated until no differences between hypothesis and SUL can be found anymore via a conformance test (i.e. during the model-based testing phase). As long as the system behaves deterministically regarding the given test inputs, all hypotheses resulting from the test-based modeling are minimal automata describing the system behavior seen so far. This is the central invariant of automata learning [53], which guarantees termination of the algorithm.

2.3   Related Work

Regression testing is an important and costly part of quality assurance in evolving software systems [48], usually requiring substantial manual effort to identify (meaningful) changes and determine regressions to test for. Hence, reducing the costs of these tests through clever automation has been a research topic for almost two decades.

Source code based methods [23] identify changes in the source code and use these as a basis for test case generation. In our scenario of a complex web-application, these methods cannot be applied easily (at least not for testing at the user level) since changed components often cannot be tested or executed separately in a meaningful way. The user-level behavior of the system is a product of the interplay of many components deployed in a JavaEE (Enterprise Edition) environment.

The user level of an application can be captured best in models. Thus model-based testing [58,60] is the testing strategy of choice in our case. Using model-based testing for regression testing is not a new idea. In [9], e.g., an approach is presented that uses model-checking to derive tests from the difference between two models. Another method defines regression tests capturing certain well-defined changes a specification model can be subject to [64].

However, as for all model-based testing approaches, they introduce a new challenge: a test model of the system is required as a basis for test case generation. The abovementioned approaches assume the existence of models. For cases in which there are no models, methods have been developed for generating models from code (e.g., [7]).

As we have discussed already, code-based methods (including generating models from code) do not work well in the scenario we envision: in general, user-level models cannot be reconstructed for large scale enterprise applications. We thus rely on a different method for acquiring models, i.e., test-based modeling [59], based on active automata learning. Active automata learning has been used successfully in a number of case studies for extracting models from running systems, e.g., for realistic telephone systems [16], the Mantis Bugtracker and a router [43],[2] communication protocol entities [1], the new biometric European passport [2], bot nets [8], a network of integrated controllers in the door of a car [52], and enterprise applications [5]. For the optimization of the test suites obtained in this fashion, there is a large body of work covering this topic already. Hence we do not discuss this here in detail. Instead we rely on the close correspondence between active automata learning and conformance testing [6].

---

[2] This case study of the router with its over 20.000 states was a first indication of the scalability of learning-based validation.

Business process models were originally seen as mere requirement artifacts and supported by tools like ARIS [49]. Lateron they became a major factor throughout the whole development process of the underlying applications. In particular with the introduction of BPMN 2.0 [41], which also claims to have sound execution semantics, business process modeling has become part of an application development process, which aims at involving the application expert throughout the complete development life-cycle.

This trend is, however, still at the beginning. One of the remaining obstacles is the actual integration of services into business processes, whose disappointing state-of-the-art is systematically discussed in [11]. This discussion reveals that only the so-called domain-specific business activities support reusability and a sufficient abstraction from technological detail in a way that allows for agile process development. However, their corresponding scripting dominated service integration process excludes systematic validation of process models.

The *higher-order modeling* [37] in general and *second-order servification* [38] in particular generalizes the typical approaches for invoking Java methods in (business) process models:

- Aristaflow [10] is designed to handle ad-hoc changes to processes at runtime and allows for static method invocation only. It is not designed to support a variability like our second-order approach.
- Engines following the BPMN 2 specification [41] like Activiti [3] and jBPM [46] can execute methods on objects in the context. In contrast to our approach this is realized as a kind of script activity, i.e., the method call is written as an expression. Input parameters as well as the return value are defined in the expression. Hence, the model is neither aware of the type of the service instance, its input parameters or the return values nor which context variables are accessed.
- The service component architecture [20] (SCA) is designed for infrastructure-oriented modeling and therefore based on a lower level whereas jABC focuses on the user-level process.

The new variability introduced by our approach has different dimensions, i.e.:

- The level of abstraction can be changed by choosing implementations that operate on different layers of a multi-layered enterprise application like, e.g., the presentation layer and the business logic layer as shown in this paper.
- The service provider can be replaced as it is postulated for service discovery facilities, e.g., in 'in silico' experiments in the field of bioinformatics [63].
- Legacy services may be exchanged with new service implementations seamlessly. In the field of testing, the same tests for both the Web service and the browser-based variant may be used, for example.
This way the preservation of behavior regarding the tests can be validated [40].

Active Continuous Quality Control (*ACQC*) [62] aims at closely monitoring and steering the evolution of applications throughout their whole life-cycle with minimum manual effort. Also here learning is employed as the basis for the required regression tests. In [40], we essentially extend ACQC to include risk analysts in order to infer comparable behavioral models as a basis for validating *system migrations* and purely *functional evolution* for *risk-based testing*. Risk analysts are provided with an abstract modeling level tailored to design test components (learning symbols) that encompass data-flow constraints reflecting a given risk profile. In terms of technical aspects the paper concentrates on the seamless integration of test components into the learning environment (Learn-Lib [32, 45]) and therefore on the code generation of test components and linking them to the learning setup. In this paper we concentrate on the higher-order test block integration [37–39] with respect to the polymorphic binding of the API of the SUL to the newest iteration of our modeling modeling framework jABC4[3], so that the underlying implementation of a test block can be exchanged without touching the models.

2.4   The OCS

We show the power of LCCT along the Online Conference Service (OCS) (see Fig. 3), an online manuscript submission and review service that is operated by Springer Business Science+Media[4]. It is realized as a multi-layer (Java) enterprise application (see Fig. 4), handling a constantly increasing amount of conferences and participants.

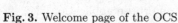
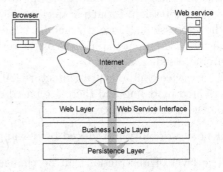

Fig. 3. Welcome page of the OCS

Fig. 4. The layered architecture of the enterprise application OCS

The main purpose of the OCS is the adequate handling of a wealth of independent but often indirectly related user interactions. Hence, completing a task may have impact on other participants or shared objects. From this point of view the OCS is a user- and context-driven reactive system with a web interface. Users can decide when they execute their tasks, which typically consist of

---

[3] http://hope.scce.info.
[4] Cf. http://springer.com.

small workflows, and in case of multiple tasks the order in which they process, or perhaps reject them. The OCS has a dynamic role system [22], meaning that in a given state different roles may have distinct action potentials. It has a high degree of freedom in choosing individual tasks and a large number of involved participants, roles (like 'author' or 'PC chair'), and interaction styles. Thus, its quality control offers a great basis for case studies for model-based testing, and active automata learning [57] (cf. also Sect. 5).

The OCS has initially only been accessible through its web interface. Lateron the requirement arose, that the OCS should be accessible headless, so that other services in the web can interoperate with the OCS. Thus it has to offer a service interface, like RESTful services [12] or web services [61].

In a well-designed multi-layer web application all validations and checks of the web layer should be double-checked in the business-logic layer. This is a prerequisite for opening the business logic via a service interface. But it is a tedious task to validate this property. We need tests that can be executed equally on both layers in order to validate conformance. As will be shown in Sect. 4, this can be elegantly realized via higher-order integration of user-level test blocks.

3   Case Study

We carried the case study out using LearnLib Studio. As in classical testing the membership queries have to be executed independently. In automata learning this is realized via a so-called *reset* that puts the SUL in a predefined state as all queries have to begin in the start state of the hypothesis automaton. In the case study the reset for every membership query creates a new conference and employs exactly one 'PC chair', 'PC member', and 'author'. Since the number of papers in a conference is negligible for the overall workflow, we furthermore allow only one paper submission per test run. The used input symbols (cf. the edge/node labels in Fig. 5) are as follows:

SP *Submit Paper*: An author submits a paper to the conference but does not provide a document file.
UD *Upload Document*: An author uploads a document file for the previously submitted paper.
DD *Download Document*: The PC Chair downloads a document file of a paper.
BD *Bidding*: A PC Member submits a bidding for a paper.
SA *Special Assignment*: The PC Chair assigns a PC Member as reviewer iff the member has bided for the paper.
SR *Submit Report*: A reviewer submits a report for a paper.
ES *End Submission*: The PC Chair stops the submissions phase. From now on it is not possible to submit any new papers. This will also start the bidding phase and all PC Members will be able to submit biddings for papers.
EU *End Upload*: The PC Chair stops the upload phase. It is no longer possible to upload documents to papers.
EB *End Bidding*: The PC Chair stops the bidding phase. Members of the program committee are no longer allowed to bid for papers.

EA *End Assignment*: The PC Chair stops the assignment phase. From now on it is not possible to assign reviewers to papers. This will also start the review phase during which all reviewers are able to submit a report to an assigned paper.

The respective symbols will be successfully executed if all prerequisites are fulfilled. E.g., a membership query with minimal length to successfully execute the symbol *Submit Report*:

$$SP \rightarrow ES \rightarrow EU \rightarrow BD \rightarrow SA \rightarrow EB \rightarrow EA \rightarrow SR$$

In this (minimal) example a report is submitted to a paper without a corresponding document. The system repeatedly warns that a document should be uploaded for every paper before the upload phase (EU) is terminated. However, the system does not prevent a user from ignoring these warnings. We will use this membership query as *running example* throughout this paper. The corresponding executable test case model is shown in Fig. 5.

4   Learning-Based Cross-Platform Conformance Testing

In this paper we combine our approach to higher-order integration [39, 40] of user-level test blocks with active automata learning [4, 5, 14, 47] in our learning framework LearnLib [32, 44, 45], to simultaneously extrapolate regular models in terms of Mealy machines on the presentation layer as well as the business logic layer (cf. Sect. 5). They are compared for equality to reveal unwanted differences.

Figure 5 illustrates the layers of abstraction in the cross-platform conformance approach. A test case model is created from an input word (i.e. a membership query selected by the learn algorithm) and an alphabet model, which consists of a selection of parameterized symbol models as described in [40]. In the following we concentrate on the polymorphic interchangeability of implementations as shown for activity 'create user'. The key to this approach is two-fold:

1. We established a 3-step top-down approach to enable users to create tests:
   (a) Test runs (membership queries) are generated, executed, and evaluated automatically via active automata learning resulting in Mealy machines (cf. layer 'Learner' in Fig. 5). Traces in such automatons represent sequences of test blocks, i.e. the *test case models*, from the user's point-of-view on the system level. Hence they are easy to understand for users.
   (b) Application experts (non-programmers) realize *symbol models* on the user-level (cf. layer 'Application Expert' in Fig. 5) in the graphical development environment jABC4 based on a simple *domain-specific language* (*DSL*). For a new learn-setup the application expert selects and parameterizes a bunch of symbol models as basis for the learner to generate test case models [40].
   (c) Testers (programmers) build technical SLGs, i.e. the *test block models*, in the jABC4 (cf. layer 'Technical Expert' in Fig. 5), abstracting from the *application programming interface* (*API*) of the system to be tested and create the aforementioned DSL for the application experts.

Test Case Models
(Learner)

Symbol Models
(Application
Expert)

Test Block Models
(Technical Expert)

Implementation
(SUL)

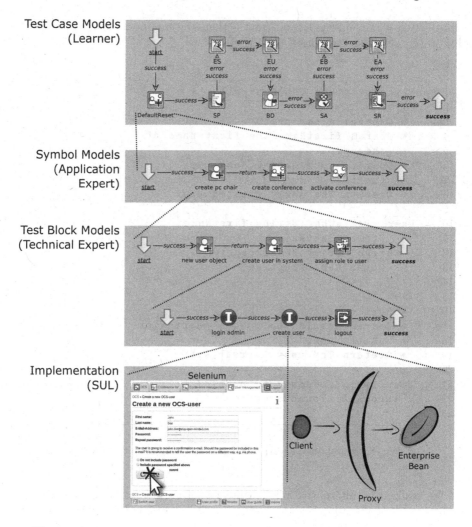

Fig. 5. The layers of abstraction in the cross-platform conformance approach.

2. Furthermore we introduce variability via higher-order service integration, in order to bridge the gap between the (RESTful) API and the browser instrumentation (cf. layer 'System Under Learning' in Fig. 5). This establishes comparability between the inferred models.

4.1 User-Level System Abstraction

The OCS is a multi-layered enterprise application, so that the presentation layer (*frontend*) is already separated from the business logic (*backend*). The API of the backend is partitioned into controller interfaces for every type of entities modeling the domain of the OCS like a *conference*, a *paper*, or a *report*. A derived controller class implements the different actions that are possible on the respective objects, e.g., 'create a user' (cf. Fig. 6).

```
1   public interface UserController {
2     /**
3      * Creates a new user.
4      * @param firstName the first name of
5      *  the user.
6      * @param lastName the last name of
7      *  the user.
8      * @return The newly created user.
9      */
10    User createUser(String firstName,
11        String lastName)
12      throws NoFirstNameException,
13        NoLastNameException;
14    // [...]
15    /**
16     * Retrieves a user.
17     * @param userId The unique identifier
18     *  of the user.
19     * @return The user to retrieve.
20     */
21    User retrieveUser(long userId)
22      throws NotFoundException;
23  }
```

Fig. 6. A simplified excerpt of the interface `UserController`

We realized an alternative implementation of these controllers, denoted by *web-test controllers*, using the web-test framework Selenium [50], which have the same impact like the backend controllers, but access the web interface as if a user would operate the OCS via a browser. Both variants of a controller implement the same controller interface.

We then use our approach to dynamic service binding (cf. Sect. 4.2) to define an SLG representing a test block in the tradition of the *integrated test environment (ITE)* [15], and define variants by parametrizing it with different service objects that implement the same API (i.e. the same controller interface).

Key to our approach is to enable application experts to write, apply and evaluate user-level test blocks, which does not require (advanced) programming skills. Since an application expert knows the domain of the application very well, but may be a non-programmer, we enable him to create test blocks as simple executable SLGs graphically. Additionally, we introduce higher-order execution semantics, allowing to realize the necessary variability in terms of dynamically exchanging the implementation of activities in a service-oriented fashion.

4.2   Higher-Order Test Block Integration

In this paper we apply the dynamic service integration [38] approach of our service-oriented development framework jABC4 to active automata learning. This provides us with the necessary variability to infer comparable models via automata learning for validating platform migrations.

Dynamic service integration is technically achieved by replacing the adapter concept (see Fig. 1) with dynamic service binding (see Fig. 2). This means that we directly bind a service in form of a Java method to an activity, denoted by a *dynamic SIB*. This is realized by considering services as *first-class objects* and therefore introducing a *type-safe second-order context* for exchange between the services of a service graph, a step reminiscent of higher-order functions in functional programming languages [51]. The type-safe second-order context is a mapping from a tuple consisting of a name (e.g. 'userController') and type information (e.g. `UserController`) to a Java object (at runtime). Each entry in this mapping is called a *context variable*. Activities may not only read and write values from context variables, but execute a method on them polymorphically. Figure 2 shows dynamic service integration. It does not require any implementation of adapters or SIB classes, as they are modeled instead as SLGs themselves on the basis of low-level services:

– Services are provided as methods of a Java class or interface (i.e. a RESTful or a Selenium service respectively), abstracting from technical details. These are integrated via dynamic SIBs in low-level graphs, which are absolutely unaware of the process models.
– A fully configured instance of a subclass of the service class or interface is read from the context as input to the corresponding dynamic SIB, and the configured method is executed via the *Java Reflection API* [13] as the control-flow reaches the activity, iff a process model is executed via an interpreter (called *Tracer* in the jABC context). The component responsible for collecting input parameters, executing the underlying service, and gathering output parameters is called *SIB container*.
– Instead of interpretation the process models may also be generated to native Java code via full-code generation omitting the need for facilitation of the Java reflection API at runtime (see also [40]).
– A bunch of low-level graphs is bundled into SIB libraries and published (as Maven[5] artifacts), so that an application expert is able to integrate them easily in high-level, coarse-grained, and domain-specific SLGs.

4.3   Dynamic SIBs

In our development environment an algorithm analyzes the public methods, public static methods and public constructors of a given set of classes of interest via reflection and presents them as dynamic SIBs to the modeler. This is realized by automatic inspection of the input parameters, return type and throwables

---

[5] http://maven.apache.org.

via reflection. The modeler can search and select them easily for use as business activities in an SLG. In advance we use the Javadoc information, in order to show the modeler information on a class and a method (see Sect. 4.6) as well as retrieve the names of method parameters, which are not available via the reflection API.

Dynamic SIBs are distinguished by means of the return type of the corresponding Java method and have different outgoing branches as described in the following. They model the control-structures *sequence*, *if-then*, and *switch*. There are three variants of dynamic SIBs:

service SIBs represent methods that have a return type other than `boolean` or enumerations. They define a 'success' branch for regular execution (i.e., no exception or error is thrown).

decision SIBs represent methods with a `boolean` return type and are used to realize if-then control-structures. Instead of a 'success' branch they have two branches corresponding to the possible return values called 'true' and 'false', respectively.

enumeration SIBs handle methods, which return Java enumerations. These SIBs realize a switch statement. Therefore they define one branch for each possible enumeration value.

All three dynamic SIB variants declare an 'exception' and an 'error' branch, for runtime exceptions and errors as well as one branch for each explicitly defined exception and error type defined[6] by the underlying service method. The return value is put into the context, if the execution returns without an error or exception. Otherwise the exception or error object is returned for further use. There is one special case: if the execution returns with a null pointer, the dedicated branch 'no result' is followed and no value is returned. There is no 'no result' branch for methods that do not have a return type[7].

The access to the context is transparent for the services. The SIB container evaluates the context and static inputs to a dynamic SIB and passes them to the service call. As the execution returns, it evaluates where to put the results to the context and which branch has to be chosen.

4.4   Execution Semantics

The procedure of a service invocation is as follows. A service instance is retrieved from the type-safe context. It may be initialized and put to the context in the SLG itself or provided as an input parameter. In general, a dynamic SIB description consists of a list of input parameters, the origin of the service instance, a list of outputs for each outgoing branch, and the method signature. Service instances as well as outputs are always read from or written to

---

[6] In Java a method can have a `throws` clause to define exceptions that may arise during execution.

[7] Methods or functions without a return type are called `void` in many *C*-derived languages like, e.g., Java.

the context, respectively. The corresponding values are represented by context variables at runtime. Besides, input parameters may be provided statically for primitive types as well as a selection of Java types supported by the jABC, e.g., `java.lang.String`, enumerations, and `java.io.File`, too. This means that a modeler can employ services and decide which input values are statically entered and which are retrieved from the shared resources (context), on-the-fly at modeling-time.

The existing interpreter, called *Tracer*, of the jABC has been enhanced for executing our higher-order processes. Interpreting (business and test) process models is in line with common practice since there exist a lot of interpreting business process engines, e.g., for BPMN 2 [41]. We realize an interpreter for our dynamic SIBs by implementing a generic adapter following the former adapter concept of the jABC. The adapter makes heavy use of the Java reflection API, which enables us to call the services dynamically although Java is a strong-typed language. This might appear as if we bypass the type discipline of Java, but on the contrary, we still have the type information, and it is exploited to check type consistency statically. Therefore type-safety and compatibility of the services are assured already at modeling-time. This is true for the service instances and for every output and input in the method signature. The types may be any Java type, i.e., they may range from a `String` or an `Integer` to domain-specific complex types like a `Paper`, `User`, or `Conference` (which are part of the entity classes modeling the domain for the OCS).

Execution of an SLG. Figure 7 shows how the execution of an SLG takes place in a process-like fashion. Please note: the term *activity* refers to a concrete node in an SLG (i.e. an instantiation of a SIB) containing all the information the modeler provided enabling to execute the service. At first the successor activity

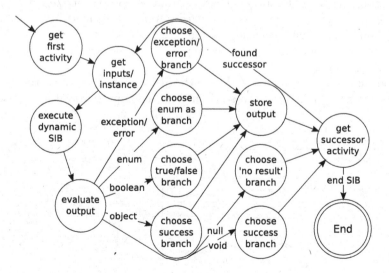

Fig. 7. Steps during execution of a dynamic SLG

of the mandatory and unique start SIB is selected (cf. 'get first activity'). Then the dynamic inputs of the activity and an instance of the service object are retrieved from the referenced context variables. Static inputs like e.g. a string are provided to the service method directly from the configuration of the activity.

As we have a type-safe second-order context, i.e., services are first-class citizens and therefore every object in the context can be used to execute methods on it. At design time the compatibility between a business activity and a context variable is checked. The same holds for reading (input parameters) and writing (output parameters) operations on a context variable. Hence it is guaranteed, that the access to context variables is type-safe.

The next step is to invoke the method (cf. 'execute dynamic SIB'). Afterwards the output is evaluated in order to select the successor SIB. The three edges labelled 'enum', 'boolean', and 'object' represent the different dynamic SIBs 'enumeration SIB', 'decision SIB', and 'service SIB'. The result is stored to context variables as configured in the activity and the corresponding branch is chosen. If the service method has a return type, but returned null, the branch 'no result' is chosen. As mentioned before service SIBs representing void methods are a special case. If such a method returns normally (i.e. without an exception or error), the branch 'success' is chosen. If the execution of the service is aborted due to an exception or error, this results in the corresponding branching as exception and error handling is part of the process modeling. The exception or error object is stored to the context variable configured in the activity. This procedure is followed until an end SIB is found.

Execution of a Dynamic SIB. During the interpretation of an SLG, several tasks have to be done. Figure 8 illustrates the involved layers and artifacts. It shows the circular flow of one SIB execution. In this event the operational flow follows two directions. First it *concretizes* from the process model level to the concrete service call. Second it is *abstracted* to the process model level again, in order to find and execute the successor service.

The concretization starts on the highest level – the service logic graph – which is executed by an interpreter. Therefore the SLG interpreter selects the current SIB node and delegates its invocation to the SIB container, which is responsible for the dynamic SIB. Here, the static inputs and inputs from the context as

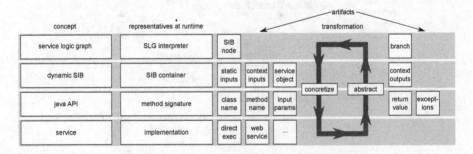

Fig. 8. Layer-model of the dynamic SIB pattern

well as the service instance itself are read in as defined in the configuration of the SIB and provided to the service. As mentioned before, the service instance (i.e. a Java object) is retrieved from the context, too. All this information is handed over to the Java API layer. A service is defined via its class name[8], the method name and its input parameters, which altogether form its signature. As services can be any implementation of the interface or superclass, they need to be invoked virtually.

After the method has returned, the abstraction phase starts. At first the return value or in the case of abnormal termination the exception or error object are retrieved. Then the value is put to the context as defined in the SIB configuration. Finally, the corresponding branch is evaluated and the successor is selected in the SLG.

4.5 Application to the Running Example

In order to show the power of the dynamic and polymorphic service integration pattern Fig. 9 depicts – along with the control-flow – the data-flow information of a technical test block model for creating a new user (cf. layer 'Test Block Models' in Fig. 5).

The first name, last name, and an instance of the user controller (cf. Listing Fig. 6) are provided via the input parameters of the SLG, represented by the output parameters of the start SIB[9]. They are stored to the respective context variables. The activity 'create user', then takes all this information and executes

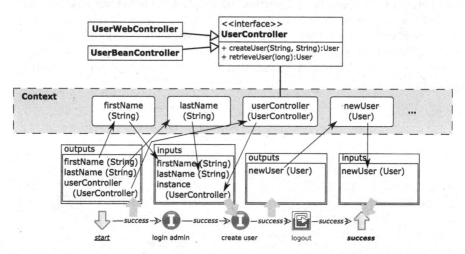

Fig. 9. The data-flow of the technical test block model in Fig. 5.

---

[8] The notion *class* may refer to a class, an interface, an enumeration as well as an annotation.

[9] The outputs of a start SIB represent the input parameters of the respective process according to the differentiation between actual and formal parameters of functions in programming languages.

the method `createUser()` on the instance of the user controller. As shown on top of the context variable 'userController', there are two implementations of this interface: the `UserWebController` (frontend) and the `UserBeanController` (backend). Depending on the instance stored to the variable at runtime, the respective method will be exectuted polymorphically.

4.6   Putting It All Together

In Fig. 10 an excerpt of the concrete execution of the example SLG in Fig. 9 is shown. At the top of the figure, a coarse overview of the execution is depicted, exhibiting the concretization and abstraction process for each invocation of a dynamic SIB.

The excerpt starts with the activity 'login admin' depicted in Fig. 9. The staircaise-shaped line represents the concretizing and abstracting phases shown in Fig. 8. After the login, the activity 'create user' is executed. A detailed view of the concrete execution of 'create user' is shown beneath via a second staircase-shaped line. The interpreter starts on the SLG layer, invoking the corresponding activity. On the next layer (i.e. 'SIB') the input parameters are evaluated as well as the `instance` parameter representing the user controller instance which will be used for the method call. The API level deals with the reflection information to select the responsible class and method to execute. Finally, on the service level, the method `createUser()` is invoked on the user controller with the respective input parameters. Hereby, the concretization is finished and the abstraction phase starts. The reflection information of the return type is evaluated on the API level. Lateron, on the SIB-level, the return value is stored to the context variable 'newUser' according to the parameterization of the activity. Since no exception has been thrown and a value has been returned, the branch 'success' is chosen and – back on the SLG-level – the successor activity 'logout' is invoked.

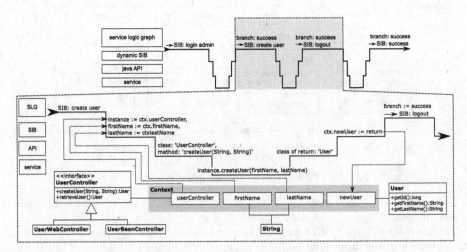

Fig. 10. A run through the different layers for a specific SIB execution

Selection of Services. There are two aspects in adding and selecting services regarding dynamic service binding. On the one hand technical services have to be provided for creating domain-specific services in form of low-level SLGs. On the other hand, these SLGs have to be found by application experts in advance, in order to design domain-specific, high-level business processes.

When we say technical services, we refer to Java methods. So in the jABC we offer a discovery mechanism that searches the current classpath for classes filtered by several criteria and present them to the modeler. The criteria can be divided into

1. class name,
2. package name,
3. class type (interface, abstract class, class, enumeration, ...), and
4. class path elements.

The resulting classes are presented in a tree, structured by their package. Their public methods (including the constructor methods) are the leaves of the tree. They can be directly integrated in a low-level SLG.

A low-level or technical SLG can be annotated with a name and a package. It is serialized to an XML-file and may be packaged in an archive (e.g., a Java archive). This archive may be imported to another jABC project (cf. Sect. 4.6). The SLGs are found automatically via a corresponding discovery mechanism and likewise are presented in a tree component. They can equally be integrated into a high-level SLG dynamically.

The Framework in Practice. In this section we show the realization of our approach in the jABC. It describes in short the workflow of creating a technical SLG with dynamic SIBs. The jABC is organized in projects representing an aggregation of related SLGs. Each project can have its own project classpath that may be dynamically enhanced by new entries at runtime. In addition, an arbitrary amount of *service trees* may be added to a project, offering the modeler technical services.

Figure 11 shows the service tree 'OCS-Services'. The Java services are organized in a tree structure via the package name. Every service class has an icon illustrating its type (e.g., an 'I' for interface as depicted in the figure). As mentioned before, the leaf nodes are the public methods, public static methods or public constructors of a service class. At the bottom of the service tree panel a quick filter by name is present, accepting wildcards. The filter considers the package name, the class name as well as the service name.

A tool tip shows up when a user hovers with his mouse over a class or method node. It presents the Javadoc information of the corresponding element. An example for service class `PaperController` and method `submitPaper()` is shown in Fig. 11. In order to provide this feature, we created a Java doclet [42], which analyzes arbitrary Java source code, generating a file with all necessary Javadoc information. The XML file has to be on the classpath, only. This means that this feature works for open source projects and services written on your own. Of course it is possible to create tools generating the XML file from Javadoc that has already been generated to HTML (e.g., if the source code is not available), for services that do not fall in any of these categories.

The user interface of the jABC (refer Fig. 12) is separated into three main areas – namely

1. the project and service browser,
2. the inspector panel, and
3. the graph canvas.

Services may be added to an SLG via drag & drop from the service tree (see Fig. 11) to the graph canvas.

The tab for SLG selection is currently chosen in the project and service browser in Fig. 12. Like for technical services it shows a tree view to the package structure of all SLGs being on the project classpath and likewise provides a quick filter by name at the bottom of the panel. An SLG may be dragged & dropped to the graph canvas like technical services and is represented as a SIB, too. Hence, such a SIB introduces hierarchy.

Below, the project and service browser in Fig. 12 the inspector panel is situated. It contains panels for SLGs and plugins of the jABC showing context information regarding the current selection in the graph canvas and in many cases allows for manipulating this information. At present the tab shows information concerning the currently edited SLG. It contains information on the package, the name, the type, and the context variables of the service logic graph. In the figure the context variable 'paperController' is selected. Therefore in the graph canvas the writing SIBs and the corresponding outgoing branches on which the variable is modified as well as the reading SIBs are highlighted. Here the start SIB retrieves the value of the context variable 'paperController' from the context of the calling SLG and writes it to .the variable 'paperController' of the second-order context. Second, the SIB `PC#submitP` reads the context variable, in order to use it as service instance calling the method `submitPaper()`.

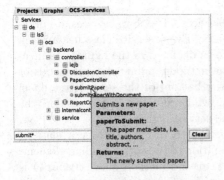

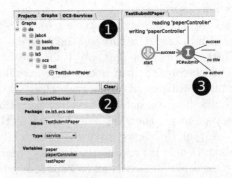

Fig. 11. OCS service tree

Fig. 12. Overview to the main areas of the jABC GUI as well as visualization of the access to context variable 'paper-Controller'

This way a modeler can keep track of the data-flow in the SLG via a local view. The read and write instructions may be set via drag & drop between the SIB and the list of variables in the inspector.

The SLG may be executed via an interpreter directly in the jABC editor. It supports common debugger features like complete as well as step-wise execution, and breakpoints. As the execution pauses, runtime information like the content of the context and the execution history is available and presented in the GUI.

4.7   Learning-Based Model Inference and Comparision

The LearnLib[10] offers a diversity of algorithms, and optimizations like paral-lelization [17] as well as an integration into the jABC framework called *LearnLib Studio*. In LearnLib Studio a modeler can graphically design a learn setup as a process model (SLG). The membership queries are realized as sequences of user-level test blocks and the test driver is an interpreter for these process models.

In order to create and perform the same learn-setup on the layer of the business-logic as well as the presentation layer of the OCS, we can use both:

- the resource optimal TTT algorithm [18], which is available in the open source LearnLib [19] and is able to generate test runs (the membership queries cf. Sect. 2.2) from a symbol alphabet to infer minimal adequate behavioral models of a system, and
- our dynamic service integration approach, enabling application experts to cre-ate higher-order user-level test blocks to be used as symbols in a learn alpha-bet.

The manual effort boils down to implementing a higher-order test blocks on the user-level (i.e. symbol models for the learn alphabet). The learn algorithm then infers behavioral models on both layers fully automatically by exchanging the implementation of the API calls to the OCS using either the frontend or the backend. The resulting Mealy automata are then compared for equality. Differences may be highlighted as traces for visual inspection.

5   Results

Figure 13 shows an excerpt of such an automaton of an OCS version with a bug in the security logic in the backend, which has been intercepted in the presentation layer. This was not apparent by inspecting the presentation layer, only. For better readability we have omitted the output symbols (namely 'success' and 'error') of the Mealy machine. Further on, the error edges (i.e., failed execution) have been removed, since they are all reflexive. This is due to the rollback mechanism of the OCS, so that errenous execution has no impact on the state of the system.

The thick line followed by a thick dotted line in Fig. 13 shows, that a member of the program committee may bid for reviewing a paper right after submission,

---

[10] LearnLib is available at http://www.learnlib.de.

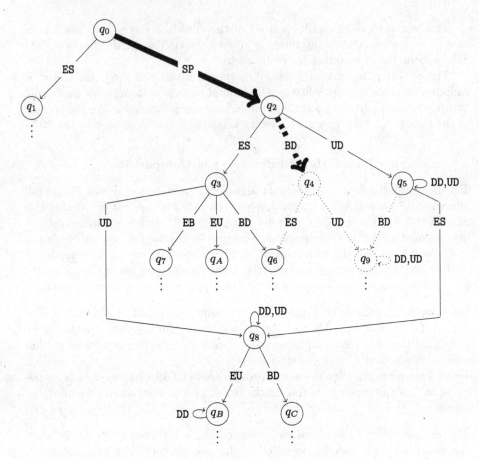

Fig. 13. Differences between learned models regarding the bidding [62].

although this should be possible after ending the submission phase (**ES**), only. This is a major issue that has also been found by our *active continuous control* (*ACQC*) approach [62], where we compare actively learned behavioral models of different system versions over time, accompanying the complete development process. By now ACQC tests the business logic only and therefore does not search for differences between frontend and backend, but it has been able to find the version which introduced the issue in the backend. Thus these are different test approaches that may complement each other. In [40] we combine ACQC with higher-order process modeling to involve risk-analysts in order to support risk-based testing. Technically, [40] focuses on the code generation of the alphabet models and integration in the LearnLib (i.e. outside of the jABC), whereas here we use LearnLib studio to execute a learn-setup in the jABC concentrating on dynamic service binding in process models via type-safe second-order contexts.

Beside some validation issues we found another major difference between frontend and backend. In the frontend there were some checks regarding the order in which conference phases may be stopped. The backend did not check that and therefore it was, e.g., possible to close the 'upload' phase before the 'submission' phase, so that only abstracts could be submitted further on.

6   Conclusion and Perspectives

In this paper we have presented learning-based cross-platform conformance testing (LCCT), an approach specifically designed to validate successful system migration. Key to our approach is the combination of (1) adequate user-level system abstraction, (2) higher-order test-block integration, and (3) learning-based automatic model inference and comparison.

LCCT employs second-order, type-safe execution semantics for (test) process models, which allows one to dynamically exchange the binding of functionality/test blocks at runtime. The impact of our approach has been illustrated along testing the conformance of the presentation layer and the business logic layer of Springer's Online Conference Service OCS during a major refactoring process that enhanced the browser-based OCS with a RESTful web service API, in order to open its services to be used by other services in the web.

Thus, our higher-order modeling approach is not specific to test processes: in an ongoing effort [34,35] we investigate its power to establish a controlled way of type-safe, agile process modeling, which can be regarded as a direct extension to the variability management solution of [21]. As the resulting approach is not limited to compile-time or modeling-time variability, process instances can be retrieved from the second-order context and evaluated at runtime. Thus it directly supports the modeling of self-adapting processes in a continuous model-driven engineering fashion [29]. Our combination of simplicity-orientation [30], domain-specific modeling [36], and continuous quality control [40,62] aims at the reliable and agile development of real-world web applications.

References

1. Aarts, F., Jonsson, B., Uijen, J.: Generating models of infinite-state communication protocols using regular inference with abstraction. In: Petrenko, A., Simão, A., Maldonado, J.C. (eds.) ICTSS 2010. LNCS, vol. 6435, pp. 188–204. Springer, Heidelberg (2010). doi:10.1007/978-3-642-16573-3_14
2. Aarts, F., Schmaltz, J., Vaandrager, F.: Inference and abstraction of the biometric passport. In: Margaria, T., Steffen, B. (eds.) ISoLA 2010. LNCS, vol. 6415, pp. 673–686. Springer, Heidelberg (2010). doi:10.1007/978-3-642-16558-0_54
3. Activiti Team: Activiti BPM Platform (2012). http://www.activiti.org/
4. Angluin, D.: Learning regular sets from queries and counterexamples. Inf. Comput. 75(2), 87–106 (1987)
5. Bauer, O., Neubauer, J., Steffen, B., Howar, F.: Reusing system states by active learning algorithms. In: Moschitti, A., Scandariato, R. (eds.) EternalS 2011. CCIS, vol. 255, pp. 61–78. Springer, Heidelberg (2012). doi:10.1007/978-3-642-28033-7_6

6. Berg, T., Grinchtein, O., Jonsson, B., Leucker, M., Raffelt, H., Steffen, B.: On the correspondence between conformance testing and regular inference. In: Cerioli, M. (ed.) FASE 2005. LNCS, vol. 3442, pp. 175–189. Springer, Heidelberg (2005). doi:10.1007/978-3-540-31984-9_14

7. Beydeda, S., Gruhn, V.: Integrating white- and black-box techniques for class-level regression testing. In: COMPSAC 2001, pp. 357–362. IEEE Computer Society, Washington, DC (2001)

8. Bossert, G., Hiet, G., Henin, T.: Modelling to simulate botnet command and control protocols for the evaluation of network intrusion detection systems. In: SAR-SSI 2011, pp. 1–8. IEEE Computer Society (2011)

9. Chen, Y., Probert, R.L., Ural, H.: Model-based regression test suite generation using dependence analysis. In: A-MOST 2007, pp. 54–62. ACM, New York (2007)

10. Dadam, P., et al.: From ADEPT to aristaflow BPM suite: a research vision has become reality. In: Rinderle-Ma, S., Sadiq, S., Leymann, F. (eds.) BPM 2009. LNBIP, vol. 43, pp. 529–531. Springer, Heidelberg (2010). doi:10.1007/978-3-642-12186-9_50

11. Doedt, M., Steffen, B.: An evaluation of service integration approaches of business process management systems. In: 2012 35th IEEE Software Engineering Workshop (SEW) (2012)

12. Fielding, R.T., Taylor, R.N.: Principled design of the modern web architecture. In: Ghezzi, C., Jazayeri, M., Wolf, A.L., (eds.) ICSE, pp. 407–416. ACM (2000)

13. Forman, I.R., Forman, N.: Java Reflection in Action (In Action series). Manning Publications Co., Greenwich (2004)

14. Gnesi, S., Margaria, T.: Formal Methods for Industrial Critical Systems: A Survey of Applications. Wiley, New York (2012)

15. Hagerer, A., Hungar, H., Margaria, T., Niese, O., Steffen, B., Ide, H.-D.: Demonstration of an operational procedure for the model-based testing of CTI systems. In: Kutsche, R.-D., Weber, H. (eds.) FASE 2002. LNCS, vol. 2306, pp. 336–339. Springer, Heidelberg (2002). doi:10.1007/3-540-45923-5_25

16. Hagerer, A., Hungar, H., Niese, O., Steffen, B.: Model generation by moderated regular extrapolation. In: Kutsche, R.-D., Weber, H. (eds.) FASE 2002. LNCS, vol. 2306, pp. 80–95. Springer, Heidelberg (2002). doi:10.1007/3-540-45923-5_6

17. Howar, F., Bauer, O., Merten, M., Steffen, B., Margaria, T.: The teachers' crowd: The impact of distributed oracles on active automata learning. In: Hähnle, R., Knoop, J., Margaria, T., Schreiner, D., Steffen, B. (eds.) ISoLA 2012, pp. 232–247. Springer, Heidelberg (2012)

18. Isberner, M., Howar, F., Steffen, B.: The TTT algorithm: a redundancy-free approach to active automata learning. In: Bonakdarpour, B., Smolka, S.A. (eds.) RV 2014. LNCS, vol. 8734, pp. 307–322. Springer, Heidelberg (2014). doi:10.1007/978-3-319-11164-3_26

19. Isberner, M., Howar, F., Steffen, B.: The open-source learnlib. In: Kroening, D., Pǎsǎreanu, C.S. (eds.) CAV 2015. LNCS, vol. 9206, pp. 487–495. Springer, Heidelberg (2015). doi:10.1007/978-3-319-21690-4_32

20. Jung, G., Margaria, T., Nagel, R., Schubert, W., Steffen, B., Voigt, H.: SCA and jABC: bringing a service-oriented paradigm to web-service construction. In: Margaria, T., Steffen, B. (eds.) ISoLA 2008. CCIS, vol. 17, pp. 139–154. Springer, Heidelberg (2008). doi:10.1007/978-3-540-88479-8_11

21. Jörges, S., Lamprecht, A.-L., Margaria, T., Schaefer, I., Steffen, B.: A constraint-based variability modeling framework. STTT **14**, 511–530 (2012)

22. Karusseit, M., Margaria, T.: A web-based runtime-reconfigurable role management service. In: 2006 2nd International Workshop on Automated Specification and Verification of Web Systems, WWV 2006, pp. 53–60. IEEE (2007)

23. Korel, B., Al-Yami, A.M.: Automated regression test generation. SIGSOFT Softw. Eng. Notes 23(2), 143–152 (1998)

24. Margaria, T.: Service is in the eyes of the beholder. IEEE Comput. 40, 33–37 (2007)

25. Margaria, T., Niese, O., Raffelt, H., Steffen, B.: Efficient test-based model generation for legacy reactive systems. In: Ninth IEEE International Proceedings of the High-Level Design Validation and Test Workshop, HLDVT 2004, pp. 95–100. IEEE Computer Society, Washington, DC (2004)

26. Margaria, T., Steffen, B.: Lightweight coarse-grained coordination: a scalable system-level approach. STTT 5(2–3), 107–123 (2004)

27. Margaria, T., Steffen, B.: Agile IT: thinking in user-centric models. In: Margaria, T., Steffen, B. (eds.) ISoLA 2008. CCIS, vol. 17, pp. 490–502. Springer, Heidelberg (2008). doi:10.1007/978-3-540-88479-8_35

28. Margaria, T., Steffen, B.: Business process modeling in the jABC: the one-thing approach. In: Handbook of Research on Business Process Modeling, pp. 1–26. IGI Global (2009)

29. Margaria, T., Steffen, B.: Continuous model-driven engineering. IEEE Comput. 42(10), 106–109 (2009)

30. Margaria, T., Steffen, B.: Simplicity as a driver for agile innovation. Computer 43(6), 90–92 (2010)

31. Margaria, T., Steffen, B.: Service-orientation: conquering complexity with XMDD. In: Hinchey, M., Koyle, L. (eds.) Conquering Complexity, pp. 217–236. Springer, London (2012)

32. Merten, M., Steffen, B., Howar, F., Margaria, T.: Next generation learnlib. In: Abdulla, P.A., Leino, K.R.M. (eds.) TACAS 2011. LNCS, vol. 6605, pp. 220–223. Springer, Heidelberg (2011). doi:10.1007/978-3-642-19835-9_18

33. Müller-Olm, M., Schmidt, D., Steffen, B.: Model-checking: a tutorial introduction. In: SAS, pp. 330–354 (1999)

34. Neubauer, J.: Higher-order process engineering. Ph.D. thesis, Technische Universität Dortmund (2014)

35. Neubauer, J.: Higher-order process engineering: the technical background. Technical report, Technische Universität Dortmund, April 2014

36. Neubauer, J., Frohme, M., Steffen, B., Margaria, T.: Prototype-driven development of web applications with DyWA. In: Margaria, T., Steffen, B. (eds.) ISoLA 2014. LNCS, vol. 8802, pp. 56–72. Springer, Heidelberg (2014). doi:10.1007/978-3-662-45234-9_5

37. Neubauer, J., Steffen, B.: Plug&play higher-order process integration. Computer (2013)

38. Neubauer, J., Steffen, B.: Second-order servification. In: Herzwurm, G., Margaria, T. (eds.) ICSOB 2013. LNBIP, vol. 150, pp. 13–25. Springer, Heidelberg (2013). doi:10.1007/978-3-642-39336-5_2

39. Neubauer, J., Steffen, B., Margaria, T.: Higher-order process modeling: product-lining, variability modeling and beyond. arXiv preprint. arXiv:1309.5143 (2013)

40. Neubauer, J., Windmüller, S., Steffen, B.: Risk-based testing via active continuous quality control. Int. J. STTT 16(5), 569–591 (2014)

41. OMG. Business Process Model and Notation (BPMN) Version 2.0 (2011). http://www.omg.org/spec/BPMN/2.0/

42. Oracle: Javadoc API. http://docs.oracle.com/javase/1.5.0/docs/guide/javadoc/doclet/spec/index.html

43. Raffelt, H., Merten, M., Steffen, B., Margaria, T.: Dynamic testing via automata learning. Int. J. STTT **11**(4), 307–324 (2009)

44. Raffelt, H., Steffen, B., Berg, T.: Learnlib: a library for automata learning and experimentation. In: FMICS 2005, pp. 62–71. ACM (2005)

45. Raffelt, H., Steffen, B., Berg, T., Margaria, T.: LearnLib: a framework for extrapolating behavioral models. Int. J. STTT **11**(5), 393–407 (2009)

46. RedHat Software - JBoss. jBPM Website (2012). http://www.jboss.org/jbpm

47. Rivest, R.L., Schapire, R.E.: Inference of finite automata using homing sequences. Inf. Comput. **103**(2), 299–347 (1993)

48. Rothermel, G., Harrold, M.J., Dedhia, J.: Regression test selection for C++ software. Softw. Test. Verif. Reliab. **10**, 77–109 (1999)

49. Scheer, A.-W., Schneider, K.: ARIS – architecture of integrated information systems. In: Bernus, P., Mertins, K., Schmidt, G. (eds.) Handbook on Architectures of Information Systems, pp. 605–623. Springer, Heidelberg (2006). doi:10.1007/3-540-26661-5_25

50. Selenium. SeleniumHQ Web application testing system, July 2015. http://seleniumhq.org/

51. Sestoft, P.: Higher-order functions. In: Sestoft, P. (ed.) Programming Language Concepts. Undergraduate Topics in Computer Science, vol. 50, pp. 77–91. Springer, London (2012)

52. Shahbaz, M., Shashidhar, K.C., Eschbach, R.: Iterative refinement of specification for component based embedded systems. In: ISSTA 2011, pp. 276–286. ACM (2011)

53. Steffen, B., Howar, F., Merten, M.: Introduction to active automata learning from a practical perspective. In: Bernardo, M., Issarny, V. (eds.) SFM 2011. LNCS, vol. 6659, pp. 256–296. Springer, Heidelberg (2011). doi:10.1007/978-3-642-21455-4_8

54. Steffen, B., Margaria, T.: METAframe in practice: design of intelligent network services. In: Olderog, E.-R., Steffen, B. (eds.) Correct System Design. LNCS, vol. 1710, pp. 390–415. Springer, Heidelberg (1999). doi:10.1007/3-540-48092-7_17

55. Steffen, B., Margaria, T., Braun, V., Kalt, N.: Hierarchical service definition. In: Annual Review of Communication, pp. 847–856. International Engineering Consortium, IEC, Chicago (1997)

56. Steffen, B., Margaria, T., Nagel, R., Jörges, S., Kubczak, C.: Model-driven development with the jABC. In: Bin, E., Ziv, A., Ur, S. (eds.) HVC 2006. LNCS, vol. 4383, pp. 92–108. Springer, Heidelberg (2007). doi:10.1007/978-3-540-70889-6_7

57. Steffen, B., Neubauer, J.: Simplified validation of emergent systems through automata learning-based testing. In: SEW 2011 (2011)

58. Tretmans, J.: Model based testing with labelled transition systems. In: Hierons, R.M., Bowen, J.P., Harman, M. (eds.) Formal Methods and Testing. LNCS, vol. 4949, pp. 1–38. Springer, Heidelberg (2008). doi:10.1007/978-3-540-78917-8_1

59. Tretmans, J.: Model-based testing and some steps towards test-based modelling. In: Bernardo, M., Issarny, V. (eds.) SFM 2011. LNCS, vol. 6659, pp. 297–326. Springer, Heidelberg (2011). doi:10.1007/978-3-642-21455-4_9

60. Utting, M., Pretschner, A., Legeard, B.: A taxonomy of model-based testing approaches. Softw. Test. Verif. Reliab. **22**(5), 297–312 (2012)

61. W3C. Web Services Description Language (WSDL) Version 2.0 (2007). http://www.w3.org/TR/2007/REC-wsdl20-20070626/

62. Windmüller, S., Neubauer, J., Steffen, B., Howar, F., Bauer, O.: Active continuous quality control. In: 16th International ACM SIGSOFT Symposium on Component-Based Software Engineering CBSE 2013, pp. 111–120. ACM SIGSOFT, New York (2013)

63. Wolstencroft, K., et al.: The (my)Grid ontology: bioinformatics service discovery. Int. J. Bioinform. Res. Appl. **3**(3), 303–325 (2007)

64. Xu, L., Dias, M., Richardson, D.: Generating regression tests via model checking. In COMPSAC 2004, pp. 336–341. IEEE Computer Society, Washington, DC (2004)

ISoLA 2014 Doctoral Symposium

Global Communication Infrastructure: Towards Standardization of Customized Projects via Profile Matching

Axel Hessenkämper[1], Barbara Steffen[2], and Steve Boßelmann[3(✉)]

[1] GEA Westfalia Separator Group GmbH, Oelde, Germany
axel.hessenkaemper@gmx.de
[2] University of Twente, Enschede, Netherlands
b.r.r.steffen@student.utwente.nl
[3] Chair of Programming Systems, TU Dortmund, Dortmund, Germany
steve.bosselmann@cs.tu-dortmund.de

Abstract. In order to increase functionality and process performance, today's and future products need a high degree of tailoring to customer needs. Key drivers are Industry 4.0 and individualized end-customer production capabilities up to *lot size one* where each product can be easily produced in small amounts and customized. This has to be accomplished under the guardrails of decreasing *time-to-market* and increasing *quality-to-market*. Additionally, within large engineering enterprises, the project engineering know-how and the capacities are distributed all over the globe. To fulfill customer requirements, the product knowledge has to be available everywhere at any time. Standardizing custom projects and high-level project configuration guidance via project profile matching are a promising step towards global engineering solutions. This paper will show and describe a first solution and simple working prototypes of a Global Communication Infrastructure (GCI) that were developed and validated based on interviews with six representatives from different industries. Here, the current state of the art regarding knowledge sharing in the different industries as well as the envisioned advantages and potential of the GCI were addressed.

Keywords: Global Communication Infrastructure (GCI) · Rule-based retrieval · Domain specific structuring · Knowledge-driven requirement specification · Enterprise-wide knowledge alignment

1 Introduction

Most manufacturing enterprises offering high-end customized products face major internal communication and alignment issues. Typically, these occur in the context of individual projects within the organization consisting of various sites, plants or other points of operation (e.g., large engineering companies and customer sites) where valuable experience and knowledge is gained. The source of these issues is that projects are conducted within a project team's horizon and are not supported by a systematic and easy-to-use way of reusing knowledge gained in the past. This is confirmed by the statement of Mr. Banus, Country Business Unit Head of Compression at Siemens

© Springer International Publishing AG 2016
A.-L. Lamprecht (Ed.): ISoLA 2012/2014, CCIS 683, pp. 83–96, 2016.
DOI: 10.1007/978-3-319-51641-7_5

Nederland NV, saying that "[Every project] has to start from an empty paper towards a package, but following a formalized procedure". Especially in customization projects, where every project team is continuously developing new product features, new processes, or handling the use of diverse materials, the knowledge alignment issue leads to the frequently occurring problem of re-inventions and re-developments [4].

1.1 Problem Definition

Referring to Nonaka-Takeuchi's SECI model [15], there are established theories of how to improve and persist organizational knowledge. However, the large organizations we visited currently do not have a satisfactory systematic way to store existing knowledge gained in previous projects. For example, files are often stored in a variety of ways, and most of the company's intellectual capital is under-used or even lost. There exist content management systems (CMS) like Livelink [8], Microsoft Share-Point [11] and ShareNet [18], but none meets and exploits the needs of global enterprises as they do not offer the possibility to globally and systematically share and search the organization's internal information and knowledge enabling employees to find the information they are looking for on time. This mismatch leads to the conclusion that organizations face the central problem of poor knowledge sharing, leading to repetitive and costly re-inventions of the wheel [4].

This problem cannot be easily overcome as the apparent loss of a subsidiary's power when providing its unique knowledge is a key managerial hurdle to introducing global knowledge-sharing in multi-national corporations [12]. At this moment with the current lack of satisfactory, systematic, and tangible ways for storing knowledge, a suitable aggregation of the distributed intellectual capital enterprise-wide in a way that can be used for concrete decision making in future projects seems almost impossible. This is confirmed by observations made in three different business scenarios as they show that the current practice of information technology is still not mature enough for a wider adoption, and that only extremely aggregated (thinned) knowledge is used [6]. Current practices are by no means a truly efficient or helpful way of storing and building upon existing knowledge and capabilities in future projects. The consequence is a significant detrimental impact on the *time* and *quality-to-market* of customized projects leading to huge amounts of redundant work.

The lack of a shared knowledge base additionally undermines any attempt to standardize the development process e.g., by standardizing the used (customized) components, approaches to specific sub-solutions, and the involved external partners and suppliers. We interviewed a representative of a leading supplier for railway control systems who stated that "not only reinventing the wheel costs unnecessary resources, but also overlooking already found and better solutions leads to inconsistent products. (…) Whenever this happens it leaves an inconsistent and unprofessional impression at the customer", a problem that needs to be overcome.

Based on the interviews with the representatives from six different industries it can be concluded that the organizations' main problem is that they often do not have a single access point for project related information that is searchable throughout the whole enterprise. This results in essential information being distributed, hidden and too context specific, leading to its limited reuse and sharing. The problem has the following internal consequences for the organizations:

1. *Misalignment:* There is little inter- and intradepartmental coordination resulting in faulty budget and timespan planning.
2. *Difficult team composition:* There is no systematic support to match project profiles with employees' competence profiles.
3. *Non-conformity:* Previously developed (project) solutions are overseen.
4. *Education of staff:* New employees need long training before they gathered sufficient knowledge.
5. *Knowledge gets lost:* On-site work remains undocumented and/or information is distributed over various types of files or sources making it unclear where to retrieve information.

1.2   State of the Art and Research Question

Today, advanced organizations use different variations of CMS and interact with these for information sharing. One interviewee stated that in their organization "the CMS allows employees to retrieve about 80% of the required information for custom projects". However, they lack a decent relevance-based prioritization. While these CMS allow querying for knowledge gained in previous projects, they lack a semantic characterization and any matching technology based on it. Being capable to 'transform' project profiles directly into information correspondingly ordered by relevance is in fact a must if one e.g. wants to adequately support sales people, informing and guiding their negotiations. Modern solutions based on corporate wikis and blogs [1, 17, 19] are still insufficient: even modern tagging, based on content analysis for unstructured content, does not deliver a knowledge profiling which is advanced enough for systematic retrieval and reuse.

The problems of the organizations' internal communication could be prevented if the experience and knowledge gained through each customization project is systematically characterized and pervasively shared throughout the whole enterprise, enabling *cross-site synergies*. Leveraging knowledge appropriately would decrease the amount of inefficient technological development and testing whilst enabling successful and adequate solutions and designs to be fine-tuned over time, becoming part of the corporate culture. As several interviewed representatives posed it, if the corporation would systematically exploit internal expertise to the fullest, quality would be improved incrementally. The impact would be especially advantageous with regard to customization, which seems to be right now a widespread weak point. As a consequence, *time-to-market* would also decrease, as similar problems would be treated more efficiently, avoiding unnecessary 'reinventions of the wheel'.

The resulting research question is therefore: How can a pervasive cross-site knowledge synergy within global enterprises be enabled by information technology? This may comprise not only used materials, but also appropriate processes, machines, best practices and gained knowledge throughout the process of the projects.

2 Research Approach

An arising question is why solutions such as ShareNet do not live up to the customers' expectations. The answer is stated in a paper by Young [20] that hints at the impossibility of globalizing knowledge making it available to all stakeholders along a products' lifecycle: the heterogeneity of the data and systems as well as the lack of coordination of the involved parties are, at least today, prohibitive. This is not only a problem of size, but also a conceptual problem, as a true integration of all this heterogeneous knowledge would require a common semantic framework and therefore a mathematical rigor absent in most of the currently proposed (ontological) knowledge representation solutions. Our proposed approach aims at such a common semantic framework and strongly bases on relevance-based prioritization.

The applied research approach which led to the current state of our research is based upon the three cycle view of design science research by Hevner [5], namely the relevance cycle, design cycle, and rigor cycle. The relevance cycle focuses on the environment to identify problems or opportunities and bridges the gap to the design science activities. That means that the identified problems or opportunities are translated into requirements which will be handled in the design cycle according to state of the art research. The rigor cycle then ensures that arising solutions are adequately based on the knowledge base of the researchers, other scientific theories/methods, and the available expertise. We went through the three cycle view two times before we evaluated the quality of the solution and its applicability through field testing, connecting the design cycle and relevance cycle in a setting that ensures a high degree of generality.

Starting point was a demand-pull for a new enterprise-wide knowledge sharing solution formulated by Axel Hessenkämper who currently works at GEA but observed the needs also during his previous employments. He described the currently unsatisfactory state of the art of storing, retrieving and finding data as well as internal knowledge organization-wide: important information is not adequately aggregated and stored and thus lost in the process, therefore the relevant stored information is very difficult to find.

Our starting hypothesis was that this problem is relevant for many different industries. We made this more explicit by considering the internal process requirements of some representative organizations and the current level of research on this field, and interviewed six representatives from different industries to validate and iterate the identified problems and its consequences.

The interviews clearly confirmed our assumption that the knowledge sharing practices present in the addressed industries are not advanced enough to fulfill the organizations' needs. In order to establish a solution we went again through the design and rigor cycle and exploited the current state of the art of research on the field of knowledge sharing systems and databases. Here, the three authors took responsibility for different aspects: Steve Boßelmann for the technical perspective, Barbara Steffen for the requirements of a successful implementation, and Axel Hessenkämper for its usability and scope of applicability. This resulted in the concept of the Global Communication Infrastructure (GCI) whose prototype we presented to our six interview partners of the first round for their feedback concerning the GCI's potential of solving their organization's problems as well as the chances of a successful introduction of the GCI in their environments.

Overall the feedback was very positive. The interviewees were convinced that if the GCI would actually work as envisioned, it would be a major breakthrough. However, they were also skeptical that its introduction in the organizations' culture would be easy as many stakeholders are not interested in actually sharing their expert knowledge, as they fear to lose importance and power. Therefore, our goal is not only to provide a highly functional GCI from the technical perspective (as described in Sect. 2.1), but also a strategy for the introduction of the GCI with top-management support which addresses the concerns of the involved stakeholders. Here, it is important to communicate that they will all benefit from the increasing efficiency. This may well involve a cultural change towards a more global thinking: A good team is much superior to a selection of individually acting experts.

2.1 Global Communication Infrastructure

The Global Communication Infrastructure (GCI) is envisioned to be seen as a CMS enhanced with essential functionality of a recommender system. In detail, it comprises the following design decisions:

1. Consider classes of production processes as the "thing" to be properly described and widely shared within an organization for the custom project business.
2. (Dynamically) establish domain-specific solutions tailored to the individually considered classes of production processes.
3. Do this in a fashion that can be organized as a product line of tailored, multi-context knowledge representation systems.

The GCI approach allows an organization to tailor the complexity of the knowledge modeling problem to the considered class of production processes, and to slowly increase its complexity at need, but in a controlled fashion. This is possible as the GCI is based on the organization's tailored knowledge-driven requirement specification meaning that searches rely on the question *What* (requirements) rather than *How* (potential solutions). This declarative querying is typical of semantic (or property-based and profile-driven) approaches, and it is the key to directly involve technologically less advanced stakeholders like outside and inside sales people. Therefore, users are any professional involved in a custom project's lifecycle, from the acquisition to the implementation and maintenance. This way of storing knowledge differs drastically from other CMS which mainly offer a single access point of information which can be searched by finding words and filtering information.

Enabled through the requirement specification, the GCI's solution eases the exchange of knowledge and experience, standardization and process optimization by enforcing **structured reporting**, combined with **rule-based retrieval mechanisms** providing links to fitting reports on prior projects ordered by relevance according to the profiles of the project and the situation.

By systematically leveraging product and process knowledge gained during customization projects throughout the product lifecycle (e.g. commissioning, service and optimization), it additionally leads to an automatic increase of standardization within the organizations, despite the focus on individual projects and customization. The GCI grows with every continued project this way enhancing the organization's retrievable intellectual capital.

Dually, it is also possible to discontinue or take out types/categories and data whenever they become obsolete due to e.g. technological discontinuities or strategic changes, ensuring that the knowledge base is kept up-to-date in *real-time*. This systematic approach to knowledge gathering, management, and reuse decreases the amount of technological development spent on re-inventing and testing. At the same time, it reduces the *time-to-market* and increases the *quality-to-market*: GCI's rule-based retrieval function helps professionals to systematically exploit the internal expertise previously gathered at other sites and plants.

As the GCI offers one source of information for the whole organization and the fact that the projects are stored based upon specific types and data describing the main project requirements all projects are searchable based upon enterprise-wide used and understood notions meaning that information is not hidden anymore. These notions are the same for all projects and products which can be described by them, so they do not differ per product category but are rather based upon their applicability for as many products as possible. An important factor is the introduction of the GCI's role-based views meaning that depending on the job and responsibility of the employee interacting with the GCI different information of previously conducted projects is shown. Based on the same specifications the same projects in the same order will be shown to the different roles, however the description will differ as for the sales person the contract details are important, while the engineer is more interested in the product specifications and details of the building process. This further leads to the advantage of overcoming the problem of high context specificity. In addition, the GCI can be seen as a seamlessly integrated educational tool which continuously trains and provides employees with topical knowledge lowering the entry hurdle for newly hired staff. Additionally, it guarantees inter- and intra-departmental alignment, as well as a match between the project team and the specific project requests.

2.2   Continuous Improvement Cycle

The GCI is intended to be itself a customized product, created as a flexible platform with all the functionalities that then need to be customized and implemented for each specific company in collaboration with their domain experts. This customization process ensures an excellent fit of the categories/requirements in the GCI with those actually present in the product portfolio of the customer. Figure 1 shows how the GCI supports a continuous improvement cycle of the organization's intellectual capital (the picture is just meant to give an impression rather than to be read in detail): Whenever the organization receives a customization request the user may start an internal search for knowledge across the previously conducted projects available in the GCI. The (customization) project is then developed and implemented leveraging this internal

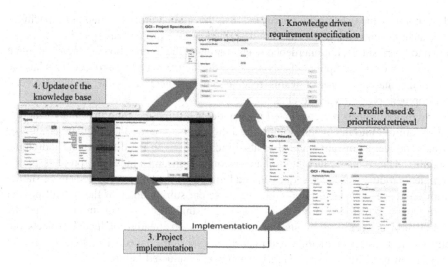

Fig. 1. GCI - continuous improvement cycle

knowledge as its foundation, and entering into the GCI the knowledge gained throughout its lifecycle. The following is the prototype description of the GCI.

The requirement specification (step 1) starts by defining the product category and determining some important primary parameters. For example, based on the choices for 'pipeline' and 'water' the system automatically asks the user to refine the water type (e.g., drink, or waste water) as this is crucial information for other requirements later on in the search (e.g. which category of material suits the given specifications). This assisted refinement functionality is possible because of the GCI's knowledge-driven requirement specification: the GCI asks the user step by step to further refine the project specifications based upon the knowledge already stored in the GCI. One can also further refine the profile (e.g. when picking 'oil', it can be specified as 'raw' or 'semi-refined'), thus adding categories the GCI does not yet comprise.

Based on the project profile the GCI retrieves a list of projects relevant to the search, ordered by relevance via the rule-based retrieval mechanism with best fitting projects marked green (step 2). The relevance is based on ontological information in terms of classifications and rules that depend on the current requirement profile.

After the subsequent step 3 in the GCI cycle in which the project is implemented, all of the gained knowledge is entered into the GCI.

Depending on whether the project handled already existing requirements or introduced new requirements the concrete way to save the knowledge differs. However, it is also very simple to introduce new requirements and specifications, as the GCI's structure can be easily adapted by the user. Thus, the GCI allows for user-level standardized enterprise-wide knowledge updates comprising structural changes and consistent archiving.

Additionally, it is envisioned that next to searching, finding and sharing the information of complete and already conducted projects the same structure can be applied to machines and processes used to develop the final product of the projects.

Here, not only the used or built parts, but also the applied processes and used machines to finalize the customized product are described. As the projects are described in detail down to every single, but interdependent component the information are included in the project profile and if required also considered during the matching process. This has the advantage that new project teams receive the complete overview of the projects' development process via one click.

As many projects are conducted in a modular fashion meaning that many different sub-solutions build the overall solution and therewith comprise the complete product or project, project teams are enabled to also find solutions to the different and individual modules. This is especially helpful in customization and innovative projects as the complete product was never requested and built before and therefore needs to be started from scratch. However, it is possible that different sub-modules of the overall project were already developed in previous projects. In this case it is not important that the overall project specification fits the specifications of already conducted projects but rather that a match of module parts can be found and connected so that the overall project can be guided even though it was never conducted before.

2.3 Technological Requirements

The emphasis on evolution and adaptation of complexity is a key proposition of the GCI. Custom projects evolve over time due to changes of requirements and general conditions or the exchange of project members and continuous development of skills and competencies. Mastering change in terms of evolving knowledge is an essential challenge in this context. So is the realization of the framework in due consideration of simplicity both as a key driver for an agile development process [9] as well as objective target regarding its usability. The GCI is envisioned to live up with this kind of evolution. The continuous improvement cycle requires transferring the knowledge generated in the project implementation phase to the existing knowledge base by means of an update. Hence, technology for this integration of knowledge throughout the continuous improvement cycle must be directed towards explicit support of evolution in a rigorous manner.

These requirements affect the knowledge base in particular. Besides essential features regarding the instantiation and provision of knowledge for an organization, it must support extension beyond simply adding data. As knowledge gained during a custom project is not predictable, it should not be limited to a pre-defined structure. Instead, new entities with new attributes as well as so far non-considered entity relations that are established during project implementation should be transferred to the knowledge base. Hence, the latter must support adaptation according to changes that eventually require the introduction of new data structures. Furthermore, this adaptation of the knowledge base should be realizable in an agile manner to expand knowledge dynamically and provide immediate availability of generated knowledge for other custom projects. But in general, maintaining a database is not a simple task, especially if the knowledge generated does not necessarily comply with the current structure of the database. It requires the technical expertise of a programmer to define and handle entity classes, attributes and inter-object associations. However, the project members that provide this knowledge generally are not technically skilled. Hence, in order to achieve an update of the knowledge base, in classical approaches the update request needs to be communicated between individuals with different expertise. Thus a common source of error is induced, known as the *semantic gap*.

We propose to overcome this hurdle by means of technology that provides both, an intuitive concept to address a wide range of users as well as a structured foundation that defines a structural basis for and enforces the correctness of generated data. The goal is to capture knowledge from stakeholders in a simple manner and use it to update the knowledge base, ideally (semi-) automatically. Any tool supporting the process of knowledge generation in the project implementation phase should provide some kind of structured approach in order to simplify subsequent knowledge transfer to the knowledge base. We propose that it must be capable of providing access to existing entities in the knowledge base and provide the functionality to create new entities with custom classification and characteristics. Furthermore, it should provide the functionality to express relations between these entities. Finally, it should be intuitive and easy to use for a broad range of stakeholders.

We are aware that creating software that combines all of these requirements is very challenging. However, we have been able to identify highly promising concepts from latest research in software engineering to be discussed in the next section.

2.4   Towards a GCI Prototype

We developed a proposal for a GCI prototype, based on requirements identified in the interviews. We have identified technology that seems to best fit these requirements and we have already applied it on selected aspects of the GCI. The next step is the actual junction by means of an integrated prototype as well as its evaluation in collaboration with our interview partners and selected project professionals.

Knowledge Base. The technical requirements we formulated emphasize the need for explicit support of evolution by means of a flexible database that supports extension in an agile manner. We found that the DyWA technology [14] is perfectly suited to instantiate, customize and grow the GCI knowledge base for an organization. DyWA provides web-based user-friendly definition of domain entities as well as their corresponding API's for a seamless integration into available business processes (e.g. Enterprise Resource Planning Systems). Furthermore, it supports modifications of the domain model at runtime and hence would enable a knowledge base to expand in an unforeseen manner. Along with its potential to easily create executable prototypes DyWA seems ideally suited to support the cultural and environmental changes mentioned above.

Knowledge Capture. The technical requirements we formulated emphasize a structured approach to support knowledge capture during the project implementation phase. The tool Blueprint has the potential to live up to these requirements. Blueprint is the prototype of a modeling tool that has been created with the *Cinco SCCE Meta Tooling Suite* [3, 13]. It allows for the design of graphical models based on a pre-defined library of model components. These components can refer to arbitrary data objects. They can be local as well as accessed remotely. In particular, the user can access data objects from an online service - such as a knowledge database - and use them to compose a graphical model. Such a model consists of several categories. Graphically, they are depicted by tiles that separate the modeling canvas. Similarly, the actual model components have a graphical representation and are mostly depicted as small rectangles with a centered label showing the component's name. This graphical representation is referred to as nodes of the model.

Nodes must be placed inside tiles. And by doing so, the represented model components are classified in respect to the categories of the model. Being classified, each component gets assigned category-specific parameters. Their values are set by the user to specify characteristics of the respective component by means of an attribute in context of the assigned category. Additionally, each two nodes can be connected to each other by edges. An edge is depicted as connection line with annotated arrowhead. As an edge represents a reference between the model components that are represented by the connected nodes, the arrowhead indicates the actual direction of this reference. Additionally, an edge can have a label showing the name of the reference that is represented.

In the context of knowledge extension, designing a model from a pre-defined library of model components generates succinct pieces of information about each component used. Along with the structural features of the model, a piece of information is either

- the classification of the component,
- a characteristic of the component or
- a reference to another component.

Despite the fact that this approach provides a powerful way of generating new knowledge based on existing data (e.g. in a knowledge base), the modeling as such is based on a series of simple modeling steps. Blueprint has been created for non-programmers and does not require any technical background or experience in handling formal models. In fact, the structure of the models based on tiles and nodes is a generalization of common models in the business domain. To name some examples, the *Business Model Canvas* [16] and related canvas-based models like the *Lean Canvas* [10] or *Strategy Sketch* [7] rely on these design rules. Being accepted tools in business strategy and widely applied in practice confirms that the systematic of this approach is adaptable for business professionals without programming skills or technical background. Actually, Blueprint is a successor of the Business Model Developer [2] and has been designed by means of abstraction and generalization of these canvas-driven approaches.

Knowledge Expansion. After having identified an appropriate technology to fulfill our requirements regarding a flexible knowledge base and motivating the use of the Blueprint prototype to capture generated knowledge, we now need to combine both tools to create an integrated solution that supports the whole GCI continuous improvement cycle. As an essential first step we created a Blueprint extension that makes it possible to access the entities managed by DyWA remotely, i.e. the knowledge base of an organization. That makes it possible to use them as model components in `Blueprint` models. In particular, the user can use existing or create new entities, arbitrary relations between them as well as custom characteristics. As the models created with `Blueprint` are clearly structured, the entities and relations created this way can be transferred to the knowledge base in an (semi-) automatic manner, assumed that an appropriate adapter has been provided. We are planning to implement this in a next step.

Exemplary Prototype. According to the approach described above, we created a prototype to illustrate the potential of the integration of `DyWA` and `Blueprint`. Processes as well as changeable components of a machine have been determined by the roles of process experts and engineering experts, respectively. In `Blueprint`, a palette lists model components to be arranged within the tiles of the model (Fig. 2). The structure of the model itself has been designed to represent the general set-up of the equipment that needs to be customized, whereas customizable components are highlighted and boxed. The modeling engineer has access to a palette that lists available components and arranges them on the canvas by means of drag and drop to the respective highlighted box.

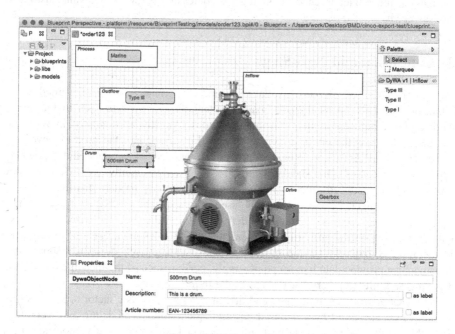

Fig. 2. Modeling toolbox

Figure 3 is showing the palette with model components to choose from as well as component-related properties and information in a respective properties view. This information is accessible during modeling whenever a model component is selected on the canvas. Provided information like the availability of a machine part could give an

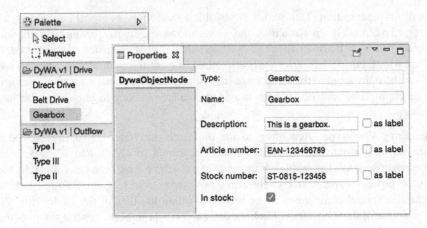

Fig. 3. Palette and property view

indication about the delivery time. If it is not on stock, a different but also process and project-fulfilling component can be chosen. Whenever a model component is exchanged, the model is checked in regards to feasibility of the relevant customer process needs.

3 Conclusion and Next Steps

The combination of globally available project experience and a simplified customization toolbox opens up new market potentials and opportunities in the standardization of highly complex customer solutions. Already accumulated knowledge can be used across the entire organization and flows back into the product development. The result is a continuous improvement process of product and customer application processes. This standardization leads to a significantly shorter processing time of orders – reduced *time-to-market* – and will improve product quality.

Next, the collected knowledge can be used in many other areas of an organization, e.g. in the sales process. Today, the delivery of a valid offer is based on many unknowns. This results primarily from not existing knowledge and lack of experience in the process required by the customer. With the approach described above the salesman can provide data like scope of supply, performance of the machine or system and process limits at a very early stage in the inquiry process.

The GCI approach is motivated and driven by simplicity as a factor of success for an innovative solution [9]. It is based on ontological domain modeling and weighted rules that allow one to retrieve best fitting project knowledge even without specific technological expertise. This intuitive approach provides a solid basis for an increased mutual and company-wide understanding. Thus the simplicity-oriented approach not only requires but also supports the corresponding cultural change towards a more global and shared thinking, which is very beneficial for the overall organizations. To explore the full potential for customer value we aim at introducing the product in a real proof of concept, in close cooperation with early adopters.

We are planning to create an integrated solution based on DyWA and Blueprint that besides accessing DyWA-managed entities from within Blueprint allows for an (semi-) automatic transfer of the knowledge represented by Blueprint models back to DyWA in order to update the knowledge base. Furthermore, we plan to evaluate the potential of this solution via concrete user-stories of a first mover that are created for different stakeholders to allow a high degree of usability for each professional target group.

Acknowledgement. We would like to thank Jarno Bredenoord, Carolina-marjolijn Klaus and Tobias Vermeer for early discussions of the business aspects, and Johannes Neubauer and Stephan Windmüller for realizing the first prototype and its visualizations (cf. Fig. 1).

References

1. Andrus, D.C.: The Wiki and the blog: toward a complex adaptive intelligence community. In: The Social Science Research Network (SSRN) (2005)
2. Boßelmann, S., Margaria, T.: Domain-specific business modeling with the business model developer. In: Margaria, T., Steffen, B. (eds.) ISoLA 2014. LNCS, vol. 8803, pp. 545–560. Springer, Heidelberg (2014). doi:10.1007/978-3-662-45231-8_45
3. Cinco SCCE Meta Tooling Suite. http://cinco.scce.info
4. Ekambaram, A., Langlo, J.A., Johansen, A.: Knowledge transfer - a study on construction projects in a Norwegian public sector organization. In: Proceedings of the 11th European Conference on Knowledge Management (2010)
5. Hevner, A.: A three cycle view of design science research. Scand. J. Inf. Syst. (2007)
6. Kasper, H., Lehrer, M., Mühlbacher, J., Müller, B.: Thinning knowledge: an interpretive field study of knowledge-sharing practices of firms in three multinational contexts. J. Manag. Inq. (2010)
7. Kraaijenbrink, J.: The Strategy Handbook: A Practical and Refreshing Guide for Making Strategy Work, Part 1. Strategy Generation. Effectual Strategy Press (2015)
8. Livelink. www.opentext.com/what-we-do/products/opentext-product-offerings-catalog/rebranded-products/livelink-is-now-part-of-the-opentext-ecm-suite
9. Margaria, T., Steffen, B.: Simplicity as a driver for agile innovation. Computer **43**(6), 90–92 (2010)
10. Maurya, A.: Running Lean. Iterate from Plan A to a Plan That Works. O'Reilly Media Inc, Sebastopol (2012)
11. Microsoft SharePoint. https://products.office.com/en-us/sharepoint/sharepoint-2013-overview-collaboration-software-features
12. Mudambi, R., Navarra, P.: Is knowledge power? Knowledge flows, subsidiary power and rent-seeking within MNCs. J. Int. Bus. Stud. (2004)
13. Naujokat, S., Lybecait, M., Kopetzki, D., Steffen, B.: Simplicity-Driven Approach to Full Generation of Domain-Specific Graphical Modeling Tools (2015, to appear)
14. Neubauer, J., Frohme, M., Steffen, B., Margaria, T.: Prototype-driven development of web applications with DyWA. In: Margaria, T., Steffen, B. (eds.) ISoLA 2014. LNCS, vol. 8802, pp. 56–72. Springer, Heidelberg (2014). doi:10.1007/978-3-662-45234-9_5
15. Nonaka, I., Takeuchi, H.: The Knowledge-Creating Company: How Japanese Companies Create the Dynamics of Innovation. Oxford University Press, Oxford (1995)
16. Osterwalder, A., Pigneur, Y.: Business Model Generation. Wiley, Hoboken (2010)

17. Remidez, H., Jones, J.B.: Developing a model for social media in project management communications. Int. J. Bus. Soc. Sci. (2012)
18. ShareNet. http://www.share-netinternational.org/
19. Stenmark, D.: Knowledge sharing through increased user participation on a corporate intranet. In: Proceedings of OKLC 2005, Bentley College, Waltham, Massachusetts, USA (2005)
20. Young, R.I.M., et al.: Manufacturing knowledge sharing in PLM: a progression towards the use of heavyweight ontologies. Int. J. Prod. Res. **45**(7), 1505–1519 (2007)

Head Pose Normalization for Recognition of Human Identities Using Color and Depth Data

Frederik Gossen[✉]

University of Limerick, Limerick, Ireland
frederik.gossen@udo.edu

Abstract. When using today's admission control systems some kind of interaction is generally required. The idea of this work was to approach identification in a contact-less manner and to improve the aspect of comfort at a relatively low loss of accuracy by recognizing people from visual facial features while they walk towards the entrance. Ideally people will not have to interact with the system deliberately. Two well known holistic methods for facial recognition are Principal Component Analysis (PCA) or Eigenfaces [17] and Local Binary Pattern Histograms [4]. Such holistic methods are expected to profit from precise alignment of face images. In this work a method will be presented to generate precisely aligned facial color and depth images. The recognition results show that both holistic methods profit significantly from these normalization steps.

Keywords: Head pose normalization · Face recognition · Admission control system · Kinect

1 Motivation

Places like fitness studios, fitness chains, swimming pools or spa are often divided into multiple areas. This allows operators to offer tickets and contracts that address their guest's needs very specifically. For instance guests will often pay extra fees to take advantage of a sauna area or other extras that are not demanded by all guests. In order to enforce the different permissions per guest an admission control system becomes necessary not only at the borders between the areas, but also at the main entrance. Today, a common approach to checking guests' identities and permissions, are RFID chips [1]. The guest will swipe his or her RFID chip through a reader in order to get identified by his or her RFID. The system will then check whether permission should be approved and will eventually open a turnstile. While this check is very reliable and yet somewhat comfortable as it happens very quickly, the guest will have to carry the RFID chip at all time. The idea of this work was to approach identification in a contact-less manner and to improve the aspect of comfort at a relatively low loss of accuracy by recognizing people from visual features. In this way guests could enter all booked areas without having to pull out their cards every time.

A.-L. Lamprecht (Ed.): ISoLA 2012/2014, CCIS 683, pp. 97–112, 2016.
DOI: 10.1007/978-3-319-51641-7_6

A guest would have to use his or her RFID card only until enough training data was collected to reliably recognize him or her in the future. In contrast to other systems, our goal is to identify people while they walk towards the entrance so they do not have to interact with our system deliberately.

This work was inspired and supported with equipment by the sysTeam GmbH from Dortmund [8].

2   Related Work

Face recognition methods can generally be divided into two categories, holistic and feature-based methods. While holistic methods process the images as a whole and pay no attention to positions of eyes or the mouth, feature-based methods aim to extract a set of features from the human face. The most popular example for holistic face recognition is Principal Component Analysis, also known as Eigenfaces [17]. This method regards the entire image as a vector and applies a dimension reduction to a space in which a search for the closest match can be performed.

Another method that can be regarded as holistic are Local Binary Patterns Histograms [4]. This method extracts Local Binary Patterns at each pixel of the image and represents them in a histogram. Using similarity metrics for histograms the search for the closest match can be performed over the histograms for all images in the training set.

An early approach of feature-based face recognition was based on geometric metrics between facial landmarks such as eyes, mouth and nose [10]. These algorithms do not provide a high degree of accuracy but geometric features can be used to narrow down the search space significantly.

Another popular feature-based approach is Elastic Bunch Graph Matching [20]. This method takes advantage of both, geometric properties of faces and local features. The method represents faces as a graph whose nodes are located at certain facial feature points such as eye corners. At each node a bunch of local features such as Gabor Wavlets is extracted from the image. The overall similarity is then computed as a weighted sum over the graph similarity and the nodes' features' similarities.

In contrast to most of the feature-based methods which evaluate local features independently, Static Bayesian Networks [9] are an approach to evaluate local features with regard to another. It was shown that the introduction of dependencies led to better results in experiments [9].

While significant progress has been made in face recognition there are still major challenges for such systems [6]. The similarity of images is not only influenced by the identity of a person but also by illumination, facial expression and head pose. Moreover, the appearance of a person can change due to make up, plastic surgery and also through natural ageing.

There exist admission control systems that take advantage of biometric technology such as FaceID [2] and FULL ID | BORDER [3]. However these systems require the user to pose in a certain position in front of a device. Moreover

FULL ID | BORDER uses biometric features as an additional verification only to improve security rather than comfort. In contrast to that, our goal is to recognize human identities while they are walking towards the entrance or the system's sensor. In this way the user's experience is most comfortable as he or she does not have to deliberately interact with our system.

3   Overview of the Proposed System

The majority of existing face recognition systems deals with 2D imagery only [19]. In many cases these images might be the only source available. However in case of an admission control system, as it will be discussed in this work 3D data can be acquired easily using an additional depth sensor. Although this entails extra costs for a second sensor, the additional depth information can lead to better recognition results as this opens up entirely new possibilities. Given all sensor information, a face recognition system is supposed to give a very specific output. This output is the predicted identity of the person that caused the observation.

Face recognition systems are often structured as a pipeline [12]. The proposed system will detect faces in a very first step. After two steps of normalization and alignment of the face images, it will match the observation to the closest identity in its database.

Face detection aims at filtering relevant information from all captured data. Only the face of a single person standing directly in front of the sensors is of any interest while the background and also other peoples' faces are irrelevant. A Haar Feature-based Cascade Classifier [13] can be used to detect position and size of faces in the 2D color imagery. Also facial feature points, such as eye corners and mouth corners will be detected as a basis for normalization steps [18] (See Fig. 1). As the depth image can be transformed into a point cloud and color information can be mapped onto it, the sensor information can be used to obtain a coloured point cloud

$$\mathcal{Q} = \left\{ (p_1, p_2, p_3, r, g, b)^T \,\middle|\, \mathbf{p} \in \mathcal{P} \wedge c(\mathbf{p}) = (r, g, b)^T \right\}. \tag{1}$$

Alignment and normalization represent a very important step of face recognition using holistic methods. This work focuses on head pose normalization in particular by generating frontal view images from the captured face information. As holistic methods process face images as a whole, the face pose is expected to have a significant impact on the system's performance.

Since these frontal view images are generally not positioned perfectly, a final step of alignment is applied. The images are translated and rotated in order to maximize horizontal symmetry.

Finally, the normalized data will be used for the recognition process. For feature extraction and feature matching, recognition methods, such as Local Binary Patterns and Principal Component Analysis [4,5] are used.

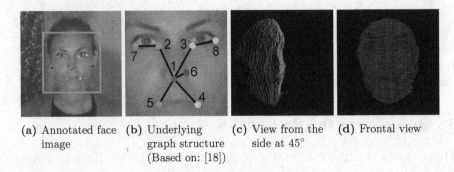

(a) Annotated face image   (b) Underlying graph structure (Based on: [18])   (c) View from the side at 45°   (d) Frontal view

Fig. 1. Facial feature points and facial point cloud (Color figure online)

4   Cropping the Face Out of the Point Cloud

So far the system captures the entire scene as a coloured point cloud Q which entails all necessary information. As the system aims to recognize individuals from their faces only any captured information which does not belong to the individual's face is unnecessary if not interfering. It is therefore necessary to filter Q to get a coloured point cloud R that contains only points that actually belong to the face.

Let $n \in \mathbb{R}^3$ be the position of the face's nose tip in space. The face can be filtered using a sphere around the nose tip of radius r_{crop} [16]. According to the size of the human face, $0.1\,m$ is an appropriate choice for the radius and leads to reasonable results as shown in Fig. 1. Given the coloured point cloud Q, the definition of the facial point cloud R follows naturally as

$$R = \left\{ q \in Q \,\middle|\, r_{crop} \geq \left| \begin{pmatrix} q_1 \\ q_2 \\ q_3 \end{pmatrix} - n \right| \right\}. \tag{2}$$

As the results show the face is filtered reasonably well from the point cloud.

5   Head Pose Normalization

When people enter an admission control system their head pose is generally unknown. Ideally they might look directly towards the system's sensors so their face is entirely visible but they might as well look somewhere completely different. As holistic methods process face images as a whole, the face pose is expected to have a significant impact on the system's accuracy. Images of different individuals where faces are oriented in the same manner show some degree of similarity. This similarity is explicitly not what an admission control system aims to classify primarily.

This step of normalization aims to represent each face under a consistent head pose. After normalization the estimated nose tip is located at **0** while the face is looking towards the positive z-axis. Moreover the y-axis is pointing to the face's top which implies the x-axis must point to the face's right side from the standpoint of an external observer. In order to transform a given facial point cloud $\mathcal{R}$ representing a face under an arbitrary head pose, translation and rotation have to be applied to each point of the cloud. As the nose tip's position $\mathbf{n} \in \mathbb{R}^3$ is already known as one of the facial feature points, translation is a subtraction by exactly this vector. The desired rotation can be expressed by a transformation matrix $\mathbf{W}$. Although this matrix is unknown at this point the transformation of the point cloud $\mathcal{R}$ into the head pose normalized point cloud $\mathcal{S}$ can already be defined as

$$\mathcal{S} = \left\{ \mathbf{W}(\mathbf{p} - (n_1, n_2, n_3, 0, 0, 0)^T) \,\middle|\, \mathbf{p} \in \mathcal{R} \right\}. \tag{3}$$

In order to determine the transformation matrix $\mathbf{W}$ the head pose in the original point cloud $\mathcal{R}$ has to be estimated in a first step. In what follows two methods will be explained to approach this problem. The result will be a target vector base $\mathcal{B} = \{\mathbf{b}^{(1)}, \mathbf{b}^{(2)}, \mathbf{b}^{(3)}\}$ indicating the head pose as explained above. For each of these methods the matrix $\mathbf{W}$ will then be a basis transformation from the original base to base $\mathcal{B}$ and can thus be expressed as

$$\mathbf{W} = \begin{pmatrix} b_1^{(1)} & b_1^{(2)} & b_1^{(3)} & 0 & 0 & 0 \\ b_2^{(1)} & b_2^{(2)} & b_2^{(3)} & 0 & 0 & 0 \\ b_3^{(1)} & b_3^{(2)} & b_3^{(3)} & 0 & 0 & 0 \\ 0 & 0 & 0 & 1 & 0 & 0 \\ 0 & 0 & 0 & 0 & 1 & 0 \\ 0 & 0 & 0 & 0 & 0 & 1 \end{pmatrix}^{-1}. \tag{4}$$

5.1 Facial Feature Points

Given the spatial information of facial feature points a solid base is given for head pose estimation. Each of these feature points is given as a vector $\mathbf{e}^{(*)} \in$

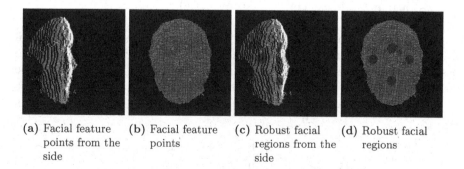

(a) Facial feature points from the side

(b) Facial feature points

(c) Robust facial regions from the side

(d) Robust facial regions

Fig. 2. Visualization of facial feature points and robust facial regions in the face cloud (Color figure online)

$\mathbb{R}^3$. Known feature points cover left and right inner eye corners ($\mathbf{e}^{(l,inner)}$ and $\mathbf{e}^{(r,inner)}$), left and right outer eye corners ($\mathbf{e}^{(l,outer)}$ and $\mathbf{e}^{(r,outer)}$) and left and right mouth corner ($\mathbf{e}^{(l,mouth)}$ and $\mathbf{e}^{(r,mouth)}$). Figure 2 highlights all of these feature points used by this method. Exploiting the properties of the human face these feature points can be used to gain information about the head pose. In a first step a horizontal vector $\mathbf{h}$ and a vertical vector $\mathbf{v}$ will be defined as a first approximation for the two base vectors $\mathbf{b}^{(1)}$ and $\mathbf{b}^{(2)}$. The vertical vector $\mathbf{v}$ will therefore indicate the direction from the face's bottom to its top while $\mathbf{h}$ indicates the direction from the face's left side to its right side from the standpoint of an external observer.

All of the given feature points are positioned symmetrical with regard to the vertical axes of the human face. The inner corner of the left eye can be matched to the inner corner of the right eye and so on. The difference of each of these pairs is already an approximation for the horizontal vector $\mathbf{h}$. In order to reduce noise due to imprecise values for single feature points one can combine multiple of these differences by taking the sum because the length of $\mathbf{h}$ is irrelevant. As mouth corners vary under facial expressions the horizontal vector $\mathbf{h}$ will be estimated as

$$\mathbf{h} = \mathbf{e}^{(r,inner)} - \mathbf{e}^{(l,inner)} + \mathbf{e}^{(r,outer)} - \mathbf{e}^{(l,outer)}. \tag{5}$$

Although the given facial feature points are not arranged symmetrical with regard to the horizontal axes of the human face, one can exploit another property of faces. While the mouth corners are located at the lower part of the human face, the eye corners represent the top part. Taking the mean of both sets of points a single reference point for both, the face's bottom and its top can be computed. Hence the vertical vector $\mathbf{v}$ can be expressed as the difference

$$\mathbf{v} = \mathbf{e}^{(upper)} - \mathbf{e}^{(lower)} \tag{6}$$

where $\mathbf{e}^{(upper)} = \dfrac{1}{4} \left(\mathbf{e}^{(l,inner)} + \mathbf{e}^{(r,inner)} + \mathbf{e}^{(l,outer)} + \mathbf{e}^{(r,outer)} \right)$

and $\mathbf{e}^{(lower)} = \dfrac{1}{2} \left(\mathbf{e}^{(l,mouth)} + \mathbf{e}^{(r,moth)} \right)$

As these first approximations $\mathbf{h}$ and $\mathbf{v}$ are not guaranteed to be orthogonal it is necessary to adjust at least one of them in order to achieve an orthogonal base. This is desirable since the face should only be rotated but it should not be stretched. The final vector base can thus be defined as

$$\mathbf{b}^{(1)} = \frac{\mathbf{h}}{|\mathbf{h}|} \tag{7}$$

$$\mathbf{b}^{(2)} = \left(\frac{\mathbf{h}}{|\mathbf{h}|} \times \frac{\mathbf{v}}{|\mathbf{v}|} \right) \times \frac{\mathbf{h}}{|\mathbf{h}|} \tag{8}$$

$$\mathbf{b}^{(3)} = \frac{\mathbf{h}}{|\mathbf{h}|} \times \frac{\mathbf{v}}{|\mathbf{v}|} \tag{9}$$

5.2 Robust Facial Regions

Although feature points can be smoothed this does not mean they are free of noise. Especially around the eyes the human face shows relatively large variation in depth which often leads to imprecise spatial information of feature points. It is therefore reasonable to find reference points that are more robust to any kind of noise and hence lead to a more accurate estimation of the head pose. Those regions might be cheeks as there is not much variation in depth but also the very center of the face provides a solid base to approximate the vertical vector.

As the head pose is initially unknown the feature points must still be used to find more robust regions in the face cloud. For the estimation of the vertical vector $\mathbf{v}$ the regions of choice are the forehead and the mouth. Both lie in the middle of eye corners respectively in the middle of mouth corners. Regions around the cheeks are used to determine the horizontal vector $\mathbf{h}$. An appropriate reference point can be found on the line between the outer eye corner and the mouth corner. In particular new reference points are derived from the existing ones. These are

$$\mathbf{e}^{(l,cheek)} = \frac{2}{3}\,\mathbf{e}^{(l,outer)} + \frac{1}{3}\,\mathbf{e}^{(l,mouth)} \tag{10}$$

$$\mathbf{e}^{(r,cheek)} = \frac{2}{3}\,\mathbf{e}^{(r,outer)} + \frac{1}{3}\,\mathbf{e}^{(r,mouth)} \tag{11}$$

$$\mathbf{e}^{(top)} = \frac{1}{4}\left(\mathbf{e}^{(l,outer)} + \mathbf{e}^{(l,inner)} + \mathbf{e}^{(r,inner)} + \mathbf{e}^{(r,outer)}\right) \tag{12}$$

$$\mathbf{e}^{(bottom)} = \frac{1}{2}\left(\mathbf{e}^{(l,mouth)} + \mathbf{e}^{(r,mouth)}\right). \tag{13}$$

So far no additional points were taken under account and the head pose estimation can hardly lead to better results than the previously proposed methods. The new reference points are only used to filter representing points out of the point cloud rather than using them directly. Unfortunately filtering using a maximal euclidean distance will not catch any point in some cases or the maximum distance must be set to a very high value. This is due to the fact that the cheek region is not necessarily on one line between the eye corner and the mouth corner.

Viewing the human face from its front the problem is caused by the differences in depth solely. A solution is to filter the regions under consideration of x- and y-coordinates only. As this assumes a face of a roughly normalized head pose it is necessary to apply the previously discussed method first.

In this way the smoothed reference points $\mathbf{e}^{(l,cheek)}$, $\mathbf{e}^{(r,cheek)}$, $\mathbf{e}^{(top)}$ and $\mathbf{e}^{(bottom)}$ can be defined as

$$\mathbf{e}'^{(*)} = mean(\{\,\mathbf{p} \in \mathcal{R} \;\big|\; r \geq \big|(e_1^{(*)}, e_2^{(*)})^T - (p_1, p_2)^T\big|\,\}). \tag{14}$$

The horizontal and the vertical vector follow naturally as

$$\mathbf{h} = \mathbf{e}'^{(r,cheek)} - \mathbf{e}'^{(l,cheek)} \tag{15}$$

$$\mathbf{v} = \mathbf{e}'^{(top)} - \mathbf{e}'^{(bottom)}. \tag{16}$$

Again the threshold value of r can be defined arbitrarily and it was chosen as 0.01 m in the experiments. Figure 2 highlights the chosen regions in the face cloud. This method of estimating the head pose is expected to be more robust against any kind of noise than using the raw facial feature points.

6   Generating Frontal View Images

As holistic methods process images rather than point clouds a conversion is necessary. In particular frontal view images are generated from the point cloud. These are an approximation of coloured images that show the face exactly from its front. In this way the normalization of the head pose will be accomplished. Given a normalized facial point cloud S the information has to be projected onto a two-dimensional image plane. As these images contain many black regions that actually belong to the face (See Fig. 3a) many pixels have to be interpolated from their neighbours. While there are many methods of inpainting unknown regions [7,15], a simple alternative is to copy the color from the closest coloured pixel. The result is shown in Fig. 3b.

It was explained how frontal view images can be generated from the point cloud using given color information per point. Through this transformation the z-coordinate of all points is ignored completely. Similarly to the color information the depth values can be mapped onto a separate frontal view image where depth information can be transformed to an intensity value in $[0, 1]$. The result is shown in Fig. 3.

The obtained frontal view images can be used for holistic face recognition directly.

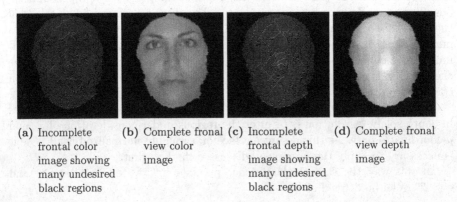

(a) Incomplete frontal color image showing many undesired black regions

(b) Complete fronal view color image

(c) Incomplete frontal depth image showing many undesired black regions

(d) Complete fronal view depth image

Fig. 3. Frontal view images based on color respectively depth information of the point cloud (Color figure online)

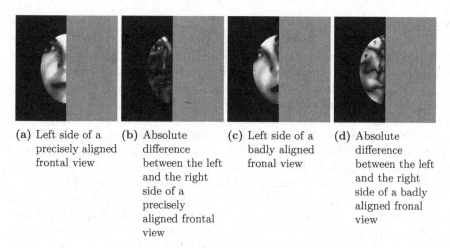

(a) Left side of a precisely aligned frontal view

(b) Absolute difference between the left and the right side of a precisely aligned frontal view

(c) Left side of a badly aligned fronal view

(d) Absolute difference between the left and the right side of a badly aligned fronal view

Fig. 4. Visualization of symmetry criterion

7   Refinement of Frontal View Images

Although the generated frontal view images are already aligned according to the head pose they are often not aligned perfectly. This is usually caused by imprecise head pose estimation. Holistic methods such as Principal Component Analysis (PCA) or Eigenfaces [17] however rely on precise alignment as they compare face images pixel wise. It is therefore expected that a further step of alignment can improve the system's recognition rate. As face pose normalization was approached using depth data in particular, the following methods will primarily take color values under account. Although the generated frontal view images do no longer allow a rotation in space, both, translation and rotation in the plane are still possible. Under the reasonable assumption that similarly rotated and translated images lead to similar error values one can apply optimization techniques such as hill-climbing to this problem [11].

Although it is a well known fact that human faces are not perfectly symmetrical, the degree of symmetry might be sufficient for precise alignment. As the axis of symmetry is supposed to be exactly in the middle of the frontal view image each pixel on the left side can be assigned a pixel on the right side. Ideally these two pixels should have approximately the same intensity.

Figure 4a shows an example of a precisely aligned face. Both, the left and the right side show a high degree of similarity which leads to a small absolute difference (See Fig. 4b). As the error function will return a comparably small value such an alignment is likely to result from the proposed optimization method. For comparison Fig. 4c shows a badly aligned image with a comparably high absolute difference (See Fig. 4d).

8   Holistic Methods

The final process of recognition is approached with one of the holistic methods, Principal Component Analysis or Local Binary Pattern Histograms.

The idea of Principal Component Analysis, also called Eigenface method, is to reduce the dimensions of face images [17]. The method regards the images as a vector of pixel intensities and transforms it to a lower dimensional subspace. While the dimension will be reduced, Principal Component Analysis aims to maintain as much information as possible. As a criterion for optimal base vectors the scattering along their directions is chosen. For more information on Principal Component Analysis at the example of face recognition see paper [5].

Another method to approach face recognition on the base of the entire images are Local Binary Pattern Histograms [4]. In a first step a so called Local Binary Pattern is obtained for each pixel of the image separately. These patterns can be represented in a histogram per image. Finally, the similarity of two images is defined as the similarity of the two generated histograms. For more details on Local Binary Patterns see paper [4].

9   Test Setup

For the experiments the Microsoft Kinect for Windows provides both, a color sensor of resolution 1280×960 pixels and a depth sensor of resolution 640×480 pixels. The Kinect was positioned at a height of $1.75\,m$ which approximately matches a person's face while standing in front of it. For the experiments people were always standing at the same distance of $1.5\,m$ in front of the sensor. The face was well illuminated by a spot light installed directly beneath the sensors. In this way relatively clear images could be achieved although the pictures were taken inside a building.

10   Data Sets

For the experiments two different data sets were used addressing the needs of the different evaluations. The first set J1 was used for the evaluation of head pose

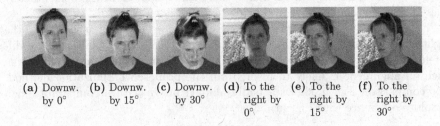

(a) Downw. by 0°   (b) Downw. by 15°   (c) Downw. by 30°   (d) To the right by 0°   (e) To the right by 15°   (f) To the right by 30°

Fig. 5. Subset of color data from set J1 (Color figure online)

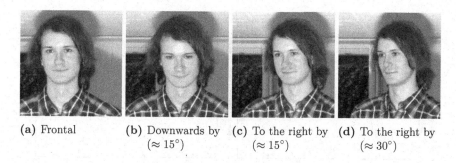

(a) Frontal   **(b)** Downwards by   **(c)** To the right by   **(d)** To the right by
(≈ 15°)   (≈ 15°)   (≈ 30°)

Fig. 6. Subset of color data from set G10 (Color figure online)

estimation while the second data set G10 will be used to evaluate the overall recognition rate of the system.

Data set J1 aims to represents a variety of defined head poses. The set contains only data from a single individual. The person was standing at a defined position in front of the sensor while the head pose was changed continuously between the captured records. During the first 31 records the face was rotated downwards from 0° to 30° starting with a face pose looking frontally towards the sensors. The second half of the data set represents horizontal rotations towards the right side of the person covering angles from 0° to 30°. Figure 5 shows a subset of the captured color data at different angles.

The second data set G10 aims to represent different individuals to evaluate the overall recognition rate of the system. The set contains data from 10 individuals under 4 different head poses. Moreover for each combination a series of 10 images were taken. Of the 4 head poses one was defined towards the sensors while another one represents a downwards rotation by approximately 15°. The 2 remaining head poses represent rotations towards the person's right hand side by 15° respectively 30°. Figure 6 shows each of the covered head poses through the example of one test person.

11   Evaluation of Head Pose Estimation

Using data set J1 the different methods for head pose normalization can be evaluated independently from the overall recognition rate. During head pose normalization for each record in J1 both, a horizontal and a vertical angle were logged indicating the horizontal respectively the vertical component of the head rotation performed by the normalization.

For the evaluation, these angles computed by the different head pose normalization methods are shown in a diagram over the actual rotation angle given by the annotation of set J1. Moreover the optimal values are indicated by a thin line of same color in the diagrams.

Head pose estimation base on raw feature points approximates the actual head pose but shows significant imprecision. The estimated angles differ from

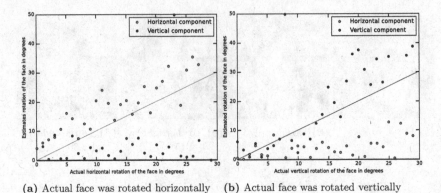

(a) Actual face was rotated horizontally   **(b)** Actual face was rotated vertically

Fig. 7. Evaluation of head pose estimation using raw feature points

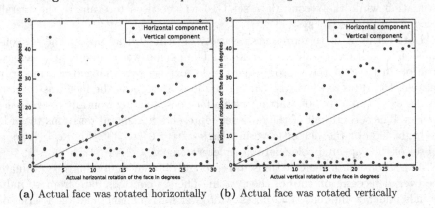

(a) Actual face was rotated horizontally   **(b)** Actual face was rotated vertically

Fig. 8. Evaluation of head pose estimation using robust facial regions

the actual angles by up to 10° for small face rotation and up to 20° for large face rotation of 15° and higher (See Fig. 7).

Regarding Fig. 8 head pose estimation based on robust regions of the face is generally more precise than the first methods. For small face rotations up to 15° the error mainly lies below 5°. For larger angles of 15° and higher the estimation of horizontally rotated faces shows an error of below 5° only. For vertically rotated faces there seems to be a systematic error. The vertical angle is generally estimated larger than it actually is. As this is a small systematic error that affects all images equally it can be ignored.

The results show that both of the proposed methods are more precise for small face rotations. Head pose estimation based on robust regions of the face was shown to be more precise. For this reason it was chosen as a basis for all further experiments.

12   Evaluation of Face Recognition

The overall recognition rate of the system was tested on data set G10 which contains 10 individuals and 400 records. The two holistic face recognition methods will be compared to another by their recognition rates on the data set. Moreover the influence of head posed estimation and refinement of alignment for frontal view images will be analysed. The system was always trained on frontally captured images while it was tested on each of the remaining 3 head poses separately.

For the following experiments robust facial regions were used to normalize the head pose as this appears to be the most accurate head pose normalization. In order to improve the alignment of the generated frontal view image the property of horizontal symmetry was exploited. The evaluation states the recognition rates in percent for 3 different head poses. Note that an evaluation on frontally captured images is meaningless as the system was trained on that data. Tables 1 and 2 state recognition rates for both face recognition methods, Principal Component Analysis and Local Binary Pattern Histograms under the influence of different normalization. "No normalization" indicates frontal view images that were generated from a facial point cloud which was not normalized at all. Hence these images will still represent rotated faces as they were captured. In contrast to that, "not aligned" indicates a head pose normalization only while the frontal face alignment was not refined afterwards. The remaining category "Aligned" includes both, head pose normalization and alignment of frontal face images.

The results show that recognition rates decrease with larger rotations of the face even if the face pose was normalized. Moreover downwards rotation seems to be not as much of a problem as side wise rotation. Head pose normalization seems to improve the recognition rates for both methods significantly. The refinement of frontal images' alignment did not bring the expected improvement.

Table 1. Recognition rates in % for Principal Component Analysis using Kinect color data

Normalization	≈15° down (%)	≈15° right (%)	≈30° right (%)
No normalization	72	38	31
Not aligned	90	70	51
Aligned	96	65	46

Table 2. Recognition rates in % for Local Binary Patterns using Kinect color data

Normalization	≈15° down (%)	≈15° right (%)	≈30° right (%)
No normalization	54	41	26
Not aligned	93	84	36
Aligned	91	80	32

Comparing both recognition methods, Principal Component Analysis often leads to better recognition rates than Local Binary Pattern Histograms in the experiment.

13 Summary

As part of this work different normalization and face recognition methods were implemented based on color and depth data. Using spatial data the focus was on normalization of the head pose but further normalization steps were proposed and evaluated.

For processing both, color and depth data both had to be merged into a coloured point cloud. Given the position of a detected face and given a set of facial feature points, the face was filtered out of the point cloud by a sphere around the nose tip. The evaluation has shown that the positions of raw feature points in space can be used for head pose estimation. However the estimated head pose was imprecise by up to $20°$ even for small head rotations. The proposed method which uses facial regions around the mouth and the cheeks for head pose estimation led to better results. For small head rotations the error was generally below $10°$. Nevertheless there is still potential to further improve head pose estimation.

After rotation of the point cloud according to the estimated head pose frontal view images were generated which aim to show the face from its front similarly to a photo. As these images were generally not aligned perfectly a method of adjusting the alignment was proposed that exploits the human face's horizontal symmetry.

Finally, the generated images were analysed with regard to the achieved recognition rates on a data set of 10 individuals under 4 different head poses. Both proposed methods, Principal Component Analysis and Local Binary Pattern Histograms were evaluated separately. The recognition rates for Principal Component Analysis reached above 90% for downwards rotated faces when all of the normalization were applied. For side wise rotations the recognition rates were significantly lower although head pose normalization was applied. Overall it seems that the head pose normalization improved the recognition results for both face recognition methods.

14 Outlook

A next step will be to extract visual features from the generated frontal faces rather than processing them with holistic methods. These could be geometric measures but also features extracted at certain facial feature points are possible [18,20]. The features can be evaluated with regard to their reliability and expressiveness. Once promising features are found, they can be combined to achieve an even stronger recognition system [9,14].

As the all of the steps discussed as part of the recognition system are still vulnerable to errors, each step can be optimized separately. The alignment of frontal view images according to face symmetry often suffers from imprecise head pose estimation. Hence improving especially this precision will likely lead to better aligned frontal view images and thus will probably improve recognition rates.

The evaluation results suffer from the small size of the data set. Recognition rates can not be compared if their difference is not significant. Hence a larger data set is necessary to improve the recognition system in the future. Moreover, the generation of frontal view images should happen while the user walks towards the device which was not yet the case during the experiments.

Finally, both, the recognition system and the RFID technology, can be put together in a way that the RFID technology is used when there was not yet enough training data collected. Eventually the user will no longer need his or her RFID card which improves the aspect of the admission control system's comfort.

References

1. Hutter, M., Schmidt, J.-M. (eds.): RFIDSec 2013. LNCS, vol. 8262. Springer, Heidelberg (2013)
2. Face id, August 2015. http://www.hanvon.com/en/products/Faceid/products/fa007.html
3. Full id border - lösungen für eine sichere und effiziente grenzkontrolle, August 2015. https://www.full-id-management.de/de/kurze-warteschlangen-und-hohe-sicherheit
4. Ahonen, T., Hadid, A., Pietikäinen, M.: Face recognition with local binary patterns. In: Pajdla, T., Matas, J. (eds.) ECCV 2004. LNCS, vol. 3021, pp. 469–481. Springer, Heidelberg (2004). doi:10.1007/978-3-540-24670-1_36
5. Belhumeur, P., Hespanha, J., Kriegman, D.: Eigenfaces vs. fisherfaces: recognition using class specific linear projection, pp. 711–720. IEEE Computer Society (1997)
6. Dantcheva, A., Ross, A., Chen, C.: Makeup challenges automated face recognition systems. SPIE Newsroom (2013)
7. Ebrahimi, M., Lunasin, E.: The Navier-Stokes-Voight Model for Image Inpainting, vol. 78. Oxford University Press, Oxford (2013). pp. 869–894
8. Göke, T., Göke, A.: Intelligentes club management systeam - software für fitness, vereine, bäder und spa, September 2014. http://www.systeam-gmbh.com/
9. Heusch, G., Marcel, S.: Face authentication with salient local features and static Bayesian network. In: Lee, S.-W., Li, S.Z. (eds.) ICB 2007. LNCS, vol. 4642, pp. 878–887. Springer, Heidelberg (2007). doi:10.1007/978-3-540-74549-5_92
10. Jafri, R., Arabnia, H.: A survey of face recognition techniques **5**, 41–68 (2009)
11. Johnson, A., Jacobson, S.: On the convergence of generalized hill climbing algorithms **119**, 37–57 (2002)
12. Li, S., Jain, A.: Handbook of Face Recognition. Springer Science & Business Media, New York (2005)
13. Lienhart, R., Kuranov, A., Pisarevsky, V.: Empirical analysis of detection cascades of boosted classifiers for rapid object detection. In: DAGM 25th Pattern Recognition Symposium, pp. 297–304 (2003)
14. Neubauer, J., Steffen, B., Margaria, T.: Higher-order process modeling: productlining, variability modeling and beyond. In: Festschrift for Dave Schmidt, pp. 259–283 (2013)

15. Telea, A.: An image inpainting technique based on the fast marching method **9**, 23–34 (2004)
16. Tu, Y., Zeng, C., Yeh, C., Huang, S., Cheng, T., Ouhyoung, M.: Real-time head pose estimation using depth map for avatar control (2011)
17. Turk, M., Pentland, A.: Eigenfaces for recognition **3**, 71–86. MIT Press (1991)
18. Uřičář, M., Franc, V., Hlaváč, V.: Detector of facial landmarks learned by the structured output SVM. In: VISAPP 2012: Proceedings of the 7th International Conference on Computer Vision Theory and Applications, vol. 1, pp. 547–556. SciTePress – Science and Technology Publications (2012)
19. Wechsler, H.: Reliable Face Recognition Methods - System Design, Implementation and Evaluation. Springer, Berlin (2007). pp. 1–329
20. Wiskott, L., Fellous, J., Krüger, N., v.d. Malsburg, C.: Face recognition by elastic bunch graph matching. In: Intelligent Biometric Techniques in Fingerprint and Face Recognition, pp. 355–396 (1999)

Guided Domain-Specific Tailoring of jABC4

Dennis Kühn[(⊠)] and Johannes Neubauer[(⊠)]

Chair for Programming Systems, Technical University Dortmund, Otto-Hahn-Str. 14,
44227 Dortmund, Germany
dennis.kuehn@udo.edu, johannes.neubauer@cs.tu-dortmund.de

Abstract. In this paper we present a new plugin for the *Java Application Building Center 4* (jABC4) that supports domain-tailoring, i.e., standardizing the way how to prepare domain-specific development environments. The new and refined features bestride templates for activities, graphical process models, and projects as well as filter views hiding information depending on the expertise of the user. This enables to shield application experts (i.e., users on the business-level) from technical details. Our domain-tailoring approach consolidates and streamlines the process of domain preparation, making it less error-prone, easy to apply, and, finally, seamlessly usable for application experts. We show the impact of guided domain-tailoring by means of the concrete process modeling domain *chainreaction*, which has already been applied in several project weeks and workshops beside others for pupils in secondary school.

1 Introduction

In a software development process it is important that application experts – who provide requirements – and technical experts – who implement the corresponding software – impair a well-known source for communication issues, the so called *semantic gap*, induced by different mindset, terminology, and experience. Neglecting this fact will in most cases result in very costly misunderstandings which increase time to market, and often even lead to project abortion [7]. The effect is even more drastic when system change becomes vital.

Business Process Modeling (BPM) has become an increasingly important attempt to decrease the semantic gap, since it involves the application expert more into the development process. The second factor is that it allows to specify the requirements in a more formal way than prose. But even *Business Process Model and Notation* (BPMN) 2.0 – which claims executability – has some shortcomings when it comes to service integration, (runtime) variability and interoperability [22].

Higher-Order Process Engineering (HOPE) [22] is an approach to tackle these three problems as it introduces (higher-order) process passing and rich features of modern programming languages like type-safety and type parameters in a hierarchical modeling environment. This combination turns out to be very powerful [23] by means of enabling *separation of concerns* [10] for efficient

© Springer International Publishing AG 2016
A.-L. Lamprecht (Ed.): ISoLA 2012/2014, CCIS 683, pp. 113–127, 2016.
DOI: 10.1007/978-3-319-51641-7_7

and conflict-free cooperation between technical experts and application experts. HOPE also elaborates the *Extreme Model Driven Design* (XMDD) [17] paradigm, by adding type-safe data-flow modeling to the in essence control-flow oriented basis. XMDD combines service orientation, model-driven design, and the end-user centeredness advocated in extreme programming as well as supports the integration of domain-specific business activities [6].

The *Java Application Building Center* (jABC) [26] is a BPM framework following the *One Thing Approach* (OTA) [16] that provides the underlying modeling infrastructure for XMDD. OTA enables all stakeholders (application experts, designers, component experts, implementers, quality assurers, ...) to closely cooperate in the development process. The current version *jABC4* has recently been released and adds support for the HOPE concepts.

Adding rich features known from modern programming languages, like type-safety, type parameters, higher-order, and full data-flow information to BPM apparently increases its complexity and technical nature, i.e., it rehashes the semantic gap. We reverse this tendency by facilitating domain-specificity. Therefore, an abstraction of the fertile features of jABC4 has to be offered, in order to supply the application experts with activities on the business level, providing a good user experience and comprehensible semantics.

Since a technical expert can provide basic activities, but has not necessarily knowledge of the domain, the resulting activities already abstract from the implementation of the underlying components, but still tend to be very generic. Therefore they are not yet remarkably beneficial for an application expert not being versed with the technical details. In contrast, an application expert needs a set of activities that are specific to the domain in which he works, so that he does not need to bother with technical details that are not part of his day-to-day work.

To bridge between the technical layer and the domain layer, an additional party is introduced: the *domain expert*. Apart from the application expert who designs business-logic in a specific domain, the domain expert rather treats *model artifacts*[1] distinctly provided by the technical experts, so that they become domain-specific and therefore usable for the application expert. In this process of tailoring the generic model artifacts to a domain the domain expert neither needs deep knowledge of the application, nor of the implementation. The primary objective is to translate from generic and technical information of model artifacts to a domain-specific and simplified terminology. This is a task that has to be done for each domain and technical solution. Our substantial experience and long history of projects [9, 12–15, 21, 24] with the jABC framework have shown that there are very diverse approaches to these issues, which are mostly ad-hoc solutions, and are often mixed with other concerns.

In this paper we present a new jABC4 plugin that supports domain-tailoring, i.e., standardizing the way how to prepare domain-specific development environments. The new and refined features (see Fig. 1) consolidate and streamline the

---

[1] model artifacts are, e.g., activities, graph models and projects.

process of domain preparation, make it less error-prone, easy to apply, and, finally, seamlessly usable for application experts:

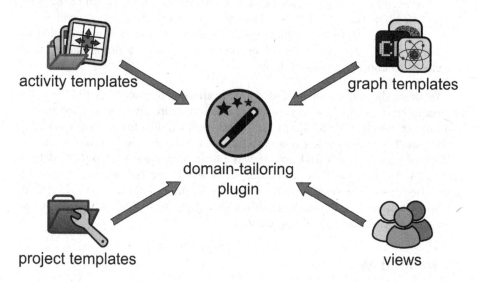

Fig. 1. The four main aspects of the jABC4 plugin for guided domain-specific tailoring.

Activity Templates. For tailored component/activity libraries a selection of generic activities is preconfigured [20] according to the given domain whereas the well-tested generic activities are reused. The following properties may be adapted:
- name and package
- names of input and output parameters
- names of outgoing edges (i.e., *branch* names)
- graphical representation (i.e., the icon of the activity)
- documentation
- type parameters (i.e., type parameters are determined to concrete types)
- data-dependencies for input- and output parameters

Graph Templates. Many *Integrated Development Environments* (IDE) offer templates for language constructs and whole classes. Therefore, support for graph templates has been added in order to reduce the recurring effort of creating process models with similarities. In addition, for a graph that implements a given interface defining the input/output parameterization we offer an automatic import of the corresponding graph definition.

Project Templates. Again following the offerings of IDEs, we support to prepare project templates which are completely preconfigured with a selection of activity libraries, graph templates, and settings (e.g., the maven[2] configuration for dependency management), that lowers the entry hurdle and tailors a jABC4 project to a given domain right from its creation.

---

[2] http://maven.apache.org.

Views. jABC4 process models, domain-specific as well as technical models, are often developed inside the same domain. In order to maintain the concept of *separation of concerns*, the *views* feature introduces a role system that allows users to adept the role of technical, domain or application expert, which can be used to annotate graph models. Users with certain roles are notified as soon as they leave their area of expertise by opening a graph model that belongs to another hierarchy level.

We show the impact of guided domain-tailoring by means of the concrete process modeling domain *chainreaction*[3], which has already been applied in several project weeks and workshops beside others for pupils in secondary school.

In Sect. 2 we position the concept of guided domain-specific tailoring in the context of existing work and how it was inspired. Section 3 introduces details on the jABC4 framework and chainreaction which use the presented concept in practice. Section 4 describes the concept's features more detailed as well as their practical application in the chainreaction domain. In Sect. 5 we present the conclusion of this concept and an outlook.

2   Related Work

The features presented in this paper are developed as a plugin for jABC4, the *Java Application Building Center* [26]. JABC is a business process modeling framework that follows the XMDD [11,17] approach. It was recently extended by the HOPE plugin which resulted in the recent version jABC4.

A recent study [6] compared the support for business activities of multiple java-based business modeling frameworks, namely *jBPM 4* and *jBPM 5* [25], *Activiti* [1], *AristaFlow* [4] and jABC. The study showed that jABC allows for an easy service integration via libraries of domain-specific business activities in contrast to the mentioned frameworks, that do not focus on this aspect. AristaFlow [3], however, is capable of creating domain-specific business activities, although these specific activities must be registered [5] in the "Activity Repository", a standalone server application which provides a repository for all activities. This makes domain preparation possible in theory but the registration and deployment to the repository do not encourage it. Especially considering support for hierarchical modeling, domain-specificity, full documentation of activities and combining data-flow with control-flow modeling, jABC is a good choice for extending its domain-tailoring capabilities. Furthermore, the fact that jABC is easily extensible by plugins [19] makes it not only reasonable but also simple to bundle the features presented in this paper as an extension to jABC4.

Although domain preparation is hardly supported in most other business process modeling tools, the use of templates for instance can be found in most IDEs [8]. New files can be generated already filled with the code for a new class, interface or enumeration, and even when creating new projects the users can

---

[3] http://hope.scce.info/chainreaction.

choose whether to create a new e.g., Java, Java EE or Android project which is already set up.

The concept of guided domain-specific tailoring bases heavily on the *Higher-Order Process Engineering* (HOPE) [22] approach, which is realized as a jABC plugin as well [19]. HOPE introduces the principle of preconfiguration for activities. The preconfiguration feature is an essential part of the preparation of domains because allowing the application experts to avoid repetitive data flow definition cuts down the effort of modeling significantly. The initial preconfiguration feature is extended in this approach by adding ways to embed prepared activities completely into the context of a domain. This is achieved by allowing a complete remake of prepared activities' documentation in order to specify their purpose inside the respective domain and strip them of the general, technical terms of their underlying non-domain-specific activity.

The PROPHETS [18] plugin for process synthesis also conceptualizes a role of a domain expert. The semantic preparation of activities by describing their behavior in a domain-specific terminology exists in PROPHETS as well but with a completely different goal. In PROPHETS, the domain expert's function is annotating activities with ontological information before the process synthesis is conducted. Whereas in this paper we propose an approach to tailor a modeling environment to the needs of a modeler and the corresponding domain. This procedure is extended here by allowing the complete redefinition of an activity's documentation which differs from the annotation of activities found in PROPHETS. Also, in this paper, the role of the domain expert is the central role in domain preparation. When the original view that only regards application level and technical level is extended by the domain expert role, this leads to a new concept that allows to reduce the semantic gap.

3 Preliminaries

This section introduces the modeling framework *jABC4* for which the concept of guided domain-specific tailoring is implemented as plugin and the *chainreaction* domain to which the domain preparations have been applied in practice.

3.1 jABC4

The domain-specific tailoring features are implemented as a plugin for jABC4 and have been realized in practice for the *chainreaction* domain. jABC4 (*Java Application Building Center*) is a business process modeling framework that is easily extensible by plugins and therefore over time gained a lot of features such as execution of process models, full-code generation as well as validation and verification of properties of models and their components.

JABC business processes are represented as graph models that depict the process flow, as seen on the right in Fig. 2. These graph models consist of a variable number of SIBs (Service Independant Building Block) that are the activities to be executed throughout the execution of the respective process. Each valid

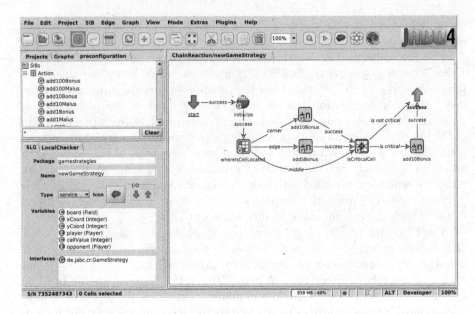

Fig. 2. A screenshot of jABC4 while modeling a chainreaction game strategy

graph model consists of exactly one entry point (*Input SIB*) and at least one exit point (*Output SIB*). Output SIBs are possible states in which the process may be terminated, so a process may have, e.g., two Output SIBs "success" and "error", one returning one or more values and the other an exception. The Input and Output SIBs define the input and output behavior of the process, i.e. the input parameters via the Input SIB and the resulting output values for every Output SIB if the respective termination state returns a result. Note that in the context of jABC, the term "workflow" is sometimes used to describe the modeled processes. Since this paper is about the optimization of the user workflow for modeling processes, this custom will not be employed throughout this text and will always refer to the actual workflow while modeling.

Data flow is handled locally in the execution context of a process. Each graph has a list of context variables (as seen on the lower left in Fig. 2) that can be read and written by the activities of the graph model. If an activity needs input of a certain type, the modeler can link the context variable to an input parameter of the activity via drag and drop and the variable's value will be used when the activity is executed. Results of activities are linked likewise and will update the value of the linked context variable. Preconfiguration of data flow eliminates the need to link certain context variables to input and output of activities, because the prepared activities are already configured to use the context variables that they have been set up to use.

When using jABC to model processes, this is always done inside of a project. Each project contains its modeled graphs and the graph and service libraries that provide the necessary activities, as seen in the upper left of Fig. 2. They may be instantiated to activities via drag and drop to the graph canvas.

3.2   Chainreaction

The *chainreaction* domain is based on the two-player game chainreaction and has been prepared for student workshops with the features presented here.

The board consists of 6 × 5 tiles called *cells* that are initially empty. Each cell has a capacity that is equal to its horizontal and vertical neighbors, i.e. corner cells have 2, edge cells 3 and center cells capacity 4. In alternating turns, the players place one token onto an empty cell or on a cell that belongs to that player. A cell belongs to a player if it has at least one token of that player. Whenever a cell has as many tokens on itself as its capacity is, it reacts and distributes all tokens to its neighbor cells. All neighbor cells therefore get an additional token and are taken over by the player who caused the reaction, including all previous tokens (see Fig. 3). If any of the neighbors now reach their capacity, they react as well, leading to a *chainreaction* that may take over many cells at once. A player wins when all opponent cells are taken over.

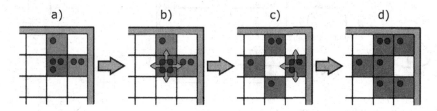

Fig. 3. An example for a chainreaction leading to the victory of the blue player. (Color figure online)

Models in the domain chainreaction represent a game strategy, which can be seen as an *Artificial Intelligence* (AI) in form of a process model. Such a game strategy is executed for every cell onto which the AI is allowed to place and that evaluates each possible cell by the decisions that the users model. During the execution an evaluation value (*cellValue*) associated with the cell is manipulated based on the boni or mali that users decide to assign under certain conditions. The *cellValue* is returned after the execution and is used by the prepared framework in order to choose, onto which cell the AI places a token by choosing the cell with the highest cell value (or, in case of a tie, randomly one of the highest rated cells).

4   Features

The central aspect of guided domain-specific tailoring is the supply of features that help domain experts prepare a domain for the application experts while using the technical activities at their hands. This is required because the application experts do not necessarily have technical background, but are the ones familiar with the details of the domain and engage in modeling the processes. At the same time the technical experts have no knowledge about the domains in which the activities will be used and therefore can only provide arbitrary, i.e., technical implementations.

The role *domain expert* is the missing link between the application and technical level. Note, that the domain expert is not presumed to be exceedingly qualified in both worlds. Instead, the domain expert treats the generic model artifacts, provided by the technical expert, which already abstract from the implementation, in order to tailor their terminology to a domain. Therefore, the domain expert neither needs deep knowledge of the application, nor of the implementation (see Fig. 4). With this, they can create prepared activities that base on the general activities but are fitted for the needs of the application experts inside a domain. This task can be extended to allow the domain experts not only the preparation of activities but also whole processes and even projects.

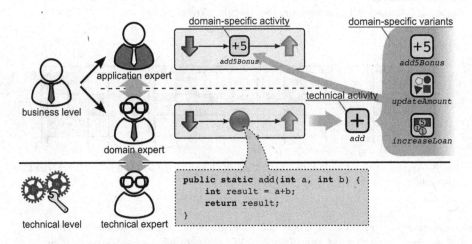

Fig. 4. The hierarchical arrangement of user levels

The aim of our approach is to provide the domain expert with a set of tools that lead the way for domain preparation since preparing a domain for a group of users not only increases the convenience of the available tools, it also allows to reduce many workflows to only a few steps. A non-prepared domain requires repetitive work, e.g. defining data-dependencies between activities again and again, although they are used in the same way in the domain. In addition these tasks are unfamiliar workflows for the users. Via domain preparation, much of the complexity found on the technical level can be hidden and the application experts can focus on a workflow that is simplified to only modeling inside their domain by stripping the technical terminology.

Expanding the ideas of BPM by an even further enhanced HOPE approach allows for an easy way to allow domain experts to provide application experts with a comprehensive and comprehensible toolset of possibilities for comfortable business process modeling. The features presented in this paper guide the domain expert in doing so by setting a standard of how the preparation of domain-specific modeling can be achieved.

4.1 Activity Templates

Without domain-specific preparation, application experts are supplied with a library of activities created by technical experts. But since technical experts might lack knowledge of the domain, activities would be technical and not suited for application experts. Preconfiguration can tackle this problem which makes it an important feature that domain experts have at hand for domain-specific tailoring. They can prepare the activities to be more suited for users unfamiliar with the technical level, so they can be provided with domain-specific, prepared activities addressing their needs.

As an example, the game strategies that are modeled inside the chainreaction domain frequently change the value of a certain context variable *cellValue* that determines the worthiness of a specific cell. This value is changed by adding boni or mali that the users decide to give for whenever certain circumstances are met by the cell. Adding a bonus or malus can be achieved by the use of the activity *Addition*, a basic activity that is not related to the domain. In order to do so, the user has to

- define the desired amount of bonus as one input parameter to *Addition*
- write *cellValue* as the other input parameter to *Addition*
- write the *Addition* activity's result back into *cellValue*

This requires many steps each time the *cellValue* should be changed and therefore becomes a very repetitive workflow due to the numerous changes made to that context variable. This is not only annoying but also error-prone.

Preparing domain-specific activities has multiple advantages as it allows a domain expert to

- predefine the data flow of the activity, partially or even completely
- rename the activity in order to specify its purpose in the domain
- rewrite the complete documentation activity so it is documented in domain-related terms that express its new purpose

This way a domain expert can use preconfiguration to create a domain-specific activity based on *Addition*, named *AddBonus* that is designed to simplify adding boni to *cellValue*.

Predefining the data flow allows the domain expert to make the activity always read *cellValue* as one parameter and write its output back into it. The result is a domain-specific activity for which users only have to set the value for the desired bonus. In addition to a generic *AddBonus* activity, the domain expert can prepare several further activities that have the bonus value predefined in the manner of *Add1Bonus*, *Add5Bonus*, *Add10Bonus*, etc. to completely erase the need to set any values, leading to an increase of user comfort and modeling speed. This example is shown in Fig. 5. The **D** icon expresses that an input parameter accepts a context variable to read from while the **S** icon symbolizes a static value that is set as a constant, in this case the prepared activity's bonus value is set to 5.

Especially when creating a set of domain-specific activities as in this case the different variants of *AddBonus*, changing the name to suite the new purpose of the activities is essential. Not only is it required for distinguishing between them but also to let them be used intuitively. Renaming and rewriting is not limited to the activity's name since it is possible to edit the entire documentation including the names of input parameters and results of activities (as shown in Fig. 5). By overwriting the technical description that is inherited by default from the underlying activity, the domain expert can completely embed the prepared activity into the context of the domain.

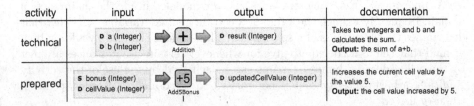

Fig. 5. The comparison of the generic *Addition* activity versus the prepared *Add5Bonus* activity.

Being able to rewrite the whole documentation to suite the terminology of the application experts greatly increases user comfort. It also clears the path for multi-language support as it is now possible to adapt to any language requirements without having to predefine the data flow again. Where having the domain expert repeat the whole preconfiguration of data flow requires a lot of effort and may lead to unintended deviation of the results, focusing only on rewriting the documentation is much faster and massively increases the maintainability. In contrast to jABC4, other tools that do not provide preconfiguration at all require a completely new activity for every different domain-specific version of an activity. Using the feature of preconfiguration allows for activities that are based upon well-tested and technically maintained activities.

4.2   Graph Templates

Process models that are developed inside a domain are likely to have a common structure that is shared between some of them. An example for this in the chainreaction domain are game strategy models. Game strategies have a specified input – namely the x and y coordinate of a cell, the current board and the current player – based on which the decisions are made. They also return an integer value determining the worthiness of the evaluated cell. Both input and output behavior is common to all valid game strategies and cannot vary. Therefore every time a user models a game strategy from scratch, he has to configure the new model's input and output behavior to match the interface definition. As a second concern, some models – including game strategies – may need to validate input or initialize default values by executing certain activities immediately at the beginning of the process. Especially when requiring many models that share a common partial process flow or need to fit a specific input and output behavior, modeling everything from scratch for each of them is time-consuming and error-prone.

The concept of templates can be found in many editors, be it as programming IDEs or textual editors. Adding a graph templates feature to jABC lets a domain expert create templates for graph models that may be partially or even completely modeled. This includes

- input and output behavior
- context variables
- process flow
- data flow
- graphical elements, e.g. in-place process documentation

Application experts are then able to one-click generate new models and only edit or complete a small portion of the generated model. Besides eliminating redundant work by allowing for a quick and convenient generation of new models, the possibility to model partial process flow makes graph templates an easy way to assure that certain contracts such as input and output behavior are satisfied for the respective activities.

4.3   Project Templates

When using jABC as a modeling framework, users work in projects that each is situated in its own domain. Every project has access to its preconfigured activities and graph template as well as the processes that were modeled inside the respective domain. The domain-tailoring that the domain expert performs mainly concentrates on the preparation of a project and using the features at hand to optimize the user's modeling workflow inside the domain lateron. But after the domain is prepared, it needs to be distributed and made accessible for the application experts.

While a project can simply be exported as an archive which can be imported back into jABC, the domain expert may also encapsulate the prepared project as a project wizard. Project wizards allow the domain expert to specify more information on the domain of the project. In contrast to the plain export that relies only on the archive name to distinguish it from other projects, the project templates feature allows for a complete description of the domain to distinguish it. Other than the export function, generated wizards are stored in a central location inside the jABC.

The greatest advantage of using wizards for the management and creation of projects is the easy access for users. In a few clicks, the correct project template can be selected from a list of all known wizards as well as their associated information. This way, the user does not need to import the project by hand but instead only selects the desired project.

Project wizards and the use of their additional description is especially useful when modeling different versions of a project due to, e.g., the use of multiple languages. The chainreaction domain, that was initially created as a domain for German workshops, is now available in two versions, each with its own description in English or German, due to the project templates feature.

4.4   Views

In jABC, a domain consists not only of graph models that are developed by application experts, such as, in chainreaction, game strategies. In fact, there may be graph models that are entirely technical such as *sort*, *equals* or, in chainreaction, the process for starting the chainreaction game. The reason for this is that in jABC, all users of the different hierarchical layers work together in the same language: process models. As a result of this, every user has access to the graphs of other hierarchy levels as well. To avoid confusion when leaving the area of expertise, we present the *Views* feature.

The concept is to not prevent users from using or viewing graphs of different hierarchy levels but to notify them when doing so. In order to evaluate if a graph belongs to the workflow of a user, this feature introduces a role system that allows users to take a role such as *Application Expert*, *Technical Expert* or *Domain Expert*. When preparing a domain, the domain expert may annotate graphs, marking specific roles that are notified of leaving the area of expertise, when users of that role open the graph model.

This way, the domain expert can tailor the domain for the need of all users and make sure they can model inside the domain and are still able to ascertain when they leave their usual workflow, all the while following the concept of separation of concerns.

5   Conclusion

We have shown how a domain expert can tailor the development environment jABC4 to a domain in a simple and guided manner that is easy to prepare for the domain expert and at the same time convenient and simple to use for the application expert. A domain expert is responsible for domain preparation of the technical basis, but does neither need deep insights into the technical realization, nor deep knowledge of the functional context. The standardized approach shields an application expert from technical details, i.e., configuring type information, type parameters and the data flow. Likewise, error-prone and repetitive modeling tasks are reduced to a minimum as the common cases are prepared completely and can just be selected in a one-click fashion. Thorough immersion into a domain is enabled by the versatile support for renaming of all elements of activities, be it package, name, input parameters, output parameters, and outcomes (i.e., names of edges denoted by *branches*) as well as adapting their appearance (i.e., changing the icon). This even enables us to realize multi-language support on the "language level".

Key to our guided approach is the *domain-tailoring*-plugin making it simple to offer templates for activities, graph process models, and projects as well as filter views for establishing responsibilities in hierarchical process models. We could see that the preparation of technical information on the one hand and the adaption to the terminology and conventions of a domain on the other hand have an ambivalent impact: First, modeling gets less costly, less technical, and more domain-specific. Second, well-tested generic technical solutions can be reused, so that changes are reflected in all of its applications and hidden technical information is still available in the models so that it can be used for validation and verification techniques. We discussed the impact by means of a concrete modeling domain for realizing strategies for computer opponents for the abstract computer board game chainreaction.

The domain-tailoring approach yields promising results and there is still a lot of potential. As we learned the templating approach from integrated development environments, we are currently investigating, whether more features of IDEs are rewarding for an *integrated modeling environment* (IME). Further on, we would like to enhance the *filter views* to hide – depending on the *role* of the current modeler – some of the technical information completely, i.e., type names, generics, or even complete input or output parameters and context variables that have been preconfigured. This would enable the application expert to focus more on his or her tasks. Another promising enhancement in this area would be a sophisticated *recommendation system* [2] that gives hints to a modeler, what he should configure or do next. E.g., after adding an *AddBonus* activity, the recommender should advice the modeler to adapt the bonus value to his needs.

References

1. Activiti Team. Activiti BPM Platform (2012). http://www.activiti.org/
2. Adomavicius, G., Tuzhilin, A.: Toward the next generation of recommender systems: a survey of the state-of-the-art and possible extensions. IEEE Trans. Knowl. Data Eng. **17**(6), 734–749 (2005)
3. AristaFlow BPM. Aristaflow website, May 2015
4. Dadam, P., et al.: From ADEPT to AristaFlow BPM suite: a research vision has become reality. In: Rinderle-Ma, S., Sadiq, S., Leymann, F. (eds.) BPM 2009. LNBIP, vol. 43, pp. 529–531. Springer, Heidelberg (2010). doi:10.1007/978-3-642-12186-9_50
5. Doedt, M.: Ph.D. thesis

6. Doedt, M., Steffen, B.: An evaluation of service integration approaches of business process management systems. In: Proceedings of the 35th Annual IEEE Software Engineering Workshop (SEW 2012). IEEE (2012)

7. El Emam, K., Koru, A.: A replicated survey of IT software project failures. Softw. IEEE **25**(5), 84–90 (2008)

8. Fields, D.K., Saunders, S.: IntelliJ IDEA in Action. Dreamtech Press, New Delhi (2006)

9. Hörmann, M., Margaria, T., Mender, T., Nagel, R., Steffen, B., Trinh, H.: The jABC approach to rigorous collaborative development of SCM applications. In: Margaria, T., Steffen, B. (eds.) ISoLA 2008. CCIS, vol. 17, pp. 724–737. Springer, Heidelberg (2008). doi:10.1007/978-3-540-88479-8_52

10. Hrsch, W.L., Lopes, C.V.: Separation of concerns. Technical report NU-CCS-95-03, College of Computer Science, Northeastern University, Boston, Massachusetts (1995)

11. Jrges, S.: Construction and Evolution of Code Generators. LNCS, vol. 7747. Springer, Heidelberg (2013)

12. Jörges, S., Steffen, B., Margaria, T.: Building code generators with Genesys: a tutorial introduction. In: Fernandes, J.M., Lämmel, R., Visser, J., Saraiva, J. (eds.) GTTSE 2009. LNCS, vol. 6491, pp. 364–385. Springer, Heidelberg (2011). doi:10. 1007/978-3-642-18023-1_10

13. Lamprecht, A.-L., Naujokat, S., Margaria, T., Steffen, B.: Semantics-based composition of EMBOSS services. J. Biomed. Semant. **2**(suppl 1), S5 (2011)

14. Margaria, T., Kubczak, C., Steffen, B., Bio-jETI: a service integration, design, and provisioning platform for orchestrated bioinformatics processes. BMC Bioinform. **9**(S-4) (2008)

15. Margaria, T., Nagel, R., Steffen, B.: jETI: a tool for remote tool integration. In: Halbwachs, N., Zuck, L.D. (eds.) TACAS 2005. LNCS, vol. 3440, pp. 557–562. Springer, Heidelberg (2005). doi:10.1007/978-3-540-31980-1_38

16. Margaria, T., Steffen, B., Modelling, B.P.: Business process modelling in the jABC: the one-thing-approach. In: Cardoso, J., van der Aalst, W. (eds.) Handbook of Research on Business Process Modeling. IGI Global, Hershey (2009)

17. Margaria, T., Steffen, B.: Service-orientation: conquering complexity with XMDD. In: Hinchey, M., Koyle, L. (eds.) Conquering Complexity, pp. 217–236. Springer, Heidelberg (2012)

18. Naujokat, S., Lamprecht, A.-L., Steffen, B.: Loose programming with PROPHETS. In: Lara, J., Zisman, A. (eds.) FASE 2012. LNCS, vol. 7212, pp. 94–98. Springer, Heidelberg (2012). doi:10.1007/978-3-642-28872-2_7

19. Naujokat, S., Neubauer, J., Lamprecht, A.-L., Steffen, B., Jrges, S., Margaria, T.: Simplicity-first model-based plug-in development. Softw.: Prac. Exp. (2013). John Wiley & Sons, Ltd.

20. Neubauer, J.: Higher-order process engineering. Ph.D. thesis, Technische Universität Dortmund (2014)

21. Neubauer, J., Margaria, T., Steffen, B.: Design for verifiability: the OCS case study. In: Formal Methods for Industrial Critical Systems: A Survey of Applications, chap. 8, pp. 153–178. Wiley-IEEE Computer Society Press, March 2013

22. Neubauer, J., Steffen, B.: Plug-and-play higher-order process integration. IEEE Comput. **46**(11), 56–62 (2013)

23. Neubauer, J., Steffen, B., Margaria, T.: Higher-order process modeling: product-lining, variability modeling and beyond. Electron. Proc. Theor. Comput. Sci. **129**, 259–283 (2013)

24. Niese, O., Steffen, B., Margaria, T., Hagerer, A., Brune, G., Ide, H.-D.: Library-based design and consistency checking of system-level industrial test cases. In: Hussmann, H. (ed.) FASE 2001. LNCS, vol. 2029, pp. 233–248. Springer, Heidelberg (2001). doi:10.1007/3-540-45314-8_17
25. RedHat Software - JBoss. jBPM Website (2012). http://www.jboss.org/jbpm
26. Steffen, B., Margaria, T., Nagel, R., Jörges, S., Kubczak, C.: Model-driven development with the jABC. In: Bin, E., Ziv, A., Ur, S. (eds.) HVC 2006. LNCS, vol. 4383, pp. 92–108. Springer, Heidelberg (2007). doi:10.1007/978-3-540-70889-6_7

Model-Driven Active Automata Learning with *LearnLib Studio*

Oliver Bauer, Johannes Neubauer$^{(\boxtimes)}$, and Malte Isberner

TU Dortmund University, 44221 Dortmund, Germany
{oliver.bauer,johannes.neubauer,malte.isberner}@cs.tu-dortmund.de

Abstract. We present our reboot of *LearnLib Studio*, formerly being a part of the *Next Generation LearnLib* (NGLL) framework for model-based construction of automata learning solutions. The new version of *LearnLib Studio* is a from-scratch re-implementation, which is based on an improved open-source realization of *LearnLib* as well as our latest version of the *jABC* framework (*jABC4*) for model-driven, service-oriented development of applications with recently added support for type-safe higher-order process modeling. Our all new version of *LearnLib Studio* provides an easy way to enable even users who do not necessarily have programming expertise to use and extend dedicated learning solutions with minimal manual effort. We illustrate the tool by applying automata learning to a concrete web service following the *Representational State Transfer* (REST) paradigm.

1 Introduction

Modern software products tend to rely on many third-party components for various functionalities, and can no longer be regarded as self-contained monolithic systems. While this service-oriented approach allows to integrate new features rapidly [35], its benefits are partially undermined by the growing complexity of these systems. This complexity, induced by the dependency on further components with their state, implementations, and communication with additional components, impedes quality assurance efforts.

The theory of software testing spawned a multitude of different techniques to tackle this complexity, and is still an evolving area of research. In the field of *model-based testing* (MBT), methodologies are exploited to automate the generation of tests from a model that expresses the desired behavior of a system.

However, the quality of results obtained by using these techniques is inherently limited by the quality of the existing models. This is a severe problem in the case of legacy software, where models are likely to be outdated, incorrect, or do not exist at all. *Test-based modeling*, also known as *active automata learning*, on the other hand, offers algorithms which generate automata models via automated testing of the target system [37], and thus has been proposed as a means of extending the applicability of model-based techniques to these cases. Building models from observed behavior makes it possible to exploit the power of

© Springer International Publishing AG 2016
A.-L. Lamprecht (Ed.): ISoLA 2012/2014, CCIS 683, pp. 128–142, 2016.
DOI: 10.1007/978-3-319-51641-7_8

formal verification techniques like model checking [7], and to continuously control the quality of a software product [29,39]. Further successful applications of active automata learning can be found in the fields of *specification mining* [34], *assume-guarantee reasoning* [8] and *risk-based testing* [30].

Applying active automata learning techniques usually involves expertise in some programming language of a framework that is used. With *LearnLib Studio* [24], we have already lowered those initial hurdles by providing a graphical development environment that allows to model a learning setup via executable process models using domain-specific activity libraries in a service-oriented manner. Along with the underlying modeling framework *Java Application Building Center* (*jABC*) [38], which allows to create software using the *Extreme Model-Driven Development* (XMDD) paradigm [22] and a rich set of additional plugins, those learning processes can be executed and the resulting models can be layouted and model checked. The realization of *LearnLib Studio* is based on *jABC3*, which has now been superseded by *jABC4* [27] following the *Higher-Order Process Engineering* (HOPE) paradigm [26], providing enhanced features like type-safety, higher-order process passing, type parameters, and dynamic service binding (i.e., adding new functionality to the modeling environment without the need to write code) and thus can realize more expressive process models. Additionally, the underlying active automata learning framework *LearnLib* has been reimplemented from scratch and published under an open-source license with a much clearer *application programming interface* (API) and improved algorithms and data structures [18].

Therefore, in this paper we present our new version of *LearnLib Studio* which allows to use active automata learning in a graphical, service-oriented way, exploiting the potential of our new open-source framework *LearnLib* [18][1] for active automata learning, as well as the latest *jABC4* [28] for service-oriented modeling and execution.

In this article, we present the following features of the new *LearnLib Studio*:

Rich Process Modeling: Irrespective of the system to be learned, the automata learning process is separated into two phases which are executed iteratively until the desired result is available. *LearnLib Studio* takes advantage of this as well as further commonalities, in order to reduce the manual effort for the standard case to a minimum. In addition, variation can be defined very locally without the necessity to touch other parts of the setup. This is realized via the rich process modeling capabilities of *jABC4*, i.e., higher-order process passing and type-safety.

Domain Tailoring: *LearnLib Studio* heavily depends on the pre-configuration features of *jABC4* [21], allowing it to be tailored to the automata learning domain. Through a set of easy-entry tutorials, an introduction to *LearnLib Studio* is provided that uses a prepared library of services and processes with predefined data-flow tailored to the domain of the respective example scenario. This approach allows to get started with *LearnLib Studio* with ease

---

[1] http://www.learnlib.de.

and shows how to prepare *LearnLib Studio* to tailor active automata learning
to concrete domains of the targeted system under learning.

Visualization: The learning algorithms have sophisticated internal data-
structures. *LearnLib Studio* offers to render them into comprehensible, com-
pact and elegant visualizations. These can be exported to different raster
and vector formats without the necessity for installing external tools like
GraphVIZ's dot tool.[2] Furthermore, the tradition of the former version of
LearnLib Studio is carried on to offer advanced statistical data collection and
presentation via an easy to use library of activities.

In addition, we show how the approach can be applied to learn a model from
an example application that serves a web service following the *Representational
State Transfer* (REST) paradigm.

Related Work. The *LibAlf* [5] framework pursues a goal similar to *LearnLib*'s: it
is an open-source framework for automata learning, written in C++. It provides
algorithms for active and passive automata learning, and for the inference of
deterministic and nondeterministic finite automata. Another such framework is
AIDE (automata-identification engine),[3] which is open-source, written in C#,
and focuses exclusively on active learning. Like *LearnLib* it contains filters (such
as a cache) to increase the practical performance of learning, and it provides
facilities for visualizing hypothesis automata through external tools. However,
both of these frameworks do not offer a stand-alone graphical (modeling) tool
such as *LearnLib Studio*.

Current business process modeling (*BPM*) approaches focus on being simple.
Therefore, variant-rich systems are not their main concern. Some BPM solutions
allow defining variants via interactive ad-hoc modeling, which is either done at
design-time [40] or at runtime [9]. Moreover, especially in the BPMN 2.0 [31]
context, the service integration process is to some extent realized via scripting
activities, which can be abused to realize run-time variability [1,32] as they can
execute methods on arbitrary objects. Here, the method call, input parameters,
and return value are defined in an expression, i.e., the model is neither aware of
the incorporated types nor which resources are accessed. The HOPE approach as
well as its incarnation *jABC4*, in contrast, supports type-safe process modeling,
runtime variability, and even self-adaptivity via higher-order process passing.

The old *LearnLib Studio* [24] combines process modeling and active automata
learning techniques, but uses the former closed-source versions of *LearnLib* and
jABC3, and is therefore constrained to their feature set.

Outline. Section 2 provides a brief introduction to active automata learning from
a theoretical perspective, while also highlighting some practical considerations.
These are further concretized in Sect. 3, where the open-source release of *Learn-
Lib* is presented. In Sect. 4, the *jABC4* framework for service-oriented construction of software systems is presented. Section 5 constitutes the main part of this

---

[2] http://www.graphviz.org/.
[3] http://aide.codeplex.com/.

article, describing a high-level, service-oriented construction of learning scenarios. Section 6 concludes the article with a presentation of future work.

2 Active Automata Learning

In 1987, Dana Angluin showed that an unknown regular language (over an *a priori* fixed alphabet Σ) can be learned in polynomial time from a so-called *Minimally Adequate Teacher* (MAT) for this language [2]. The *teacher* needs to be able to respond to two types of queries coming from a *learner*:

- *Membership queries* (MQs) consist of a word $w \in \Sigma^*$, and represent the question of whether w is contained in the unknown regular language $\mathcal{L}$ to be learned (i.e., "is $w \in \mathcal{L}$?").
- *Equivalence queries* (EQs) consist of a conjectured *deterministic finite automaton* (DFA) $\mathcal{H}$ ("hypothesis"), and are answered either with a success message indicating that the hypothesis model accepts exactly the target language $\mathcal{L}$, or with a *counterexample*, i.e., a word from the symmetric difference of the language accepted by the hypothesis and the target language.

Most learning algorithms interacting with a MAT can be separated into two phases, which are iterated until the unknown language is learned. In a *hypothesis construction phase*, an automaton is built by posing membership queries. This phase is followed by a *hypothesis validation phase*, in which the hypothesis is subjected to an equivalence query, which may either return success (in which case the learning terminates), or returns a counterexample if the hypothesis is not correct. Incorporating the counterexample into the hypothesis is then done in another iteration of the hypothesis construction phase, which again is followed by a validation phase and so on.

During the last decades a lot of research has been done to improve the L^* algorithm presented by Angluin. Improvements range from optimizations in the way counterexamples are processed in L^* (cf. e.g. [15,19]), to totally revised data structures minimizing redundancy in bookkeeping of answers from the Teacher [13,20].

The approach of *active automata learning*, where a learner is able to *actively* ask queries in order to gain knowledge, has been extended to learn a broad range of automata like *nondeterministic finite automata* (NFA) [4], *Mealy machines* [11,36] *register automata* [16] or *workflow Petri nets* [10].

In this paper we focus on the inference of *Mealy machines*, which have been proven as an adequate model for expressing the behavior of reactive systems [37]. The step from learning regular languages (or DFA) to learning Mealy machines is pretty straightforward: in principle, one only needs to replace the Boolean response of a membership query, indicating whether or not a word is part of the target language, with a string response indicating the output of the target system for the given input word. For formal definitions and further details on the theoretical aspects of learning Mealy machines, we refer the reader to [37].

Practical Aspects. Using active automata learning for inferring models of realistic systems requires overcoming a number of hurdles. The main challenge is to realize a minimally adequate teacher for the target system (also called *System Under Learning*, SUL), i.e., implementing a facility that can answer both membership and equivalence queries. This facility, which makes a real system accessible to the learner, is usually referred to as a *test driver*.

Realizing membership queries may at first seem straightforward: each input symbol corresponds to a certain action that can be executed on the SUL (e.g., a method invocation or a service call). When performing a membership query, the sequence of these actions, represented by the input word, can simply be executed, and the resulting output can be returned to the learner. However, a challenge is that the theoretical framework requires *independent execution* of membership queries: two membership queries may not influence each other. In other words, a facility for *resetting* the system is required. This, naturally, is an application-specific task. Approaches range from starting from a specific snapshot of a system for each query, resetting via homing sequences [33], to providing fresh entities [3,37].

Equivalence queries pose far bigger problems: automatically checking that an inferred model completely and correctly describes an SUL would, in general, require a model of the SUL itself, the absence of which however is the reason for applying automata learning in the first place. If the system is a "true" black box, then it is generally impossible to make any statements about the behavior of the system apart from the finite fragment exercised during learning. A common approach is to approximate equivalence queries using membership queries, for instance by random sampling, or conformance testing methods such as the W-method [6]. However, these approaches may miss errors in the model, and any kind of guarantees (such as correctness of the model under the assumption that the number of states of the target system is bounded by a certain value, as guaranteed by the W-method) usually come at the cost of an exponential number of membership queries.

To manage the huge amount of tests when learning real systems, one approach is to use filter techniques that work between a learning algorithm and the SUL. Those may range from a simple caching facility to more sophisticated approaches that allow exploiting domain-specific knowledge to reduce the number of membership queries [3,14]. Again, we refer the reader to [37] for more information on the practical aspects of automata learning.

3   LearnLib

The *LearnLib* framework is an open-source library for active automata learning. *LearnLib* contains many active automata learning algorithms, such as Anguin's L^* [2], but also some that were newly developed. Most algorithms come in two versions, one for learning DFA and one for learning Mealy machines. Additionally, some algorithms for other types of models (such as NFA [4]) exist. These learning algorithms are complemented by a rich infrastructure facilitating the practical implementation of automata learning setups, such as optimizing filters or (approximative) equivalence tests.

The current, open-source version of *LearnLib* is a complete re-implementation of former closed-source versions. It improves on these by providing a more modern and usable API, considerably higher performance [17], and a generally richer feature set in terms of both learning algorithms and supporting infrastructure. An additional major change over the previous versions is that the implementation of automaton models has been factored out to a separate library, called *AutomataLib*. *AutomataLib* is a standalone library for various types of finite-state machine models (such as DFA or Mealy machines) and graphs, and contains many automata-related algorithms, e.g., for minimization of finite-state machines, or for checking equivalence and bisimulation. Both *LearnLib* and *AutomataLib* are distributed via the Maven[4] Central repository, lowering the hurdles of integrating them with other (Java-based) software to a minimum.

Mapper Architecture. In practical applications, it is often desirable to conceptually separate between *abstract* input symbols, such as the symbolic name of a service, and *concrete* input symbols, containing the information to actually perform the service call, such as session identifiers. *LearnLib* realizes this separation by providing a *mapper* component. The main idea of this component is depicted in Fig. 1: Realizations of the Mapper interface translate abstract input symbols AI (i.e., $a \in \Sigma$) to concrete input symbols CI (e.g., a service call) executed on the SUL. The SUL responds to the concrete input with a concrete output CO (i.e., a return value or an exception), which will then be translated to an abstract output symbol AO (i.e., $o \in \Gamma$). In this process of concretization and abstraction, only the abstract level is visible to the learner, and only the concrete level is visible to the SUL.

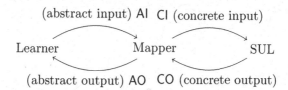

Fig. 1. Generic mapper component of *LearnLib*

Main Learning Loop. Listing 1 shows the main learning loop, consisting of the hypothesis construction (Lines 2 and 6) and hypothesis validation (Line 5) phases. The `learner` poses its membership queries to the teacher (not shown in this listing, as it is instantiated in the *configuration phase*), until a hypothesis can be obtained using `getHypothesisModel`. The *equivalence oracle* `eqOracle` realizes an approximate equivalence query by posing membership queries to

---

[4] http://maven.apache.org.

```
1   // configuration phase omitted
2   learner.startLearning();
3   do {
4     hyp = learner.getHypothesis();
5     if ((ce = eqOracle.findCounterexample(hyp, alphabet)) != null) {
6       learner.refineHypothesis(ce);
7     }
8   } while (ce != null);
```

Listing 1. A simple learning loop with *LearnLib*

the teacher, and checking the hypothesis automaton against the answers to these queries. The learning algorithm will refine its hypothesis until no further counterexamples are found (i.e., until the `findCounterexample` method returns `null`).

4   Java Application Building Center

The *Java Application Building Center* (*jABC*) [38] is a framework for service-oriented construction of applications. It has a long and successful tradition that started in 1995. Its extensible nature promoted the development of a rich set of plugins and extensions. These add support for code generation, execution semantics, synthesis, scientific workflows and many more [25].

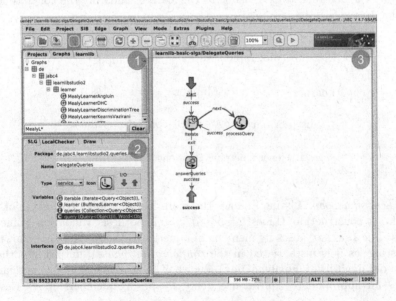

Fig. 2. User interface of *jABC* 4

One group of users that the *jABC* addresses are application experts with possibly little to no programming expertise, or even people without any technical background. Through its service-oriented approach, in combination with ideas from the extreme programming methodology and model-driven design, *jABC* follows the *eXtreme Model Driven Design* (XMDD) principle [23] which allows to integrate application experts into the development cycle of software construction.

Figure 2 depicts the jABC user interface in its current iteration *jABC4*, which adds support for type-safe modeling, type parameters, dynamic service binding, and even higher-order process modeling. The user interface is divided into the following three areas:

Browser Area: Activities (i.e., graphical components representing services and processes) are organized in a tree-like structure, sorted by their packages and names. Figure 2 shows available learning algorithms that are made available from *LearnLib*. They can be instantiated by dragging and dropping them onto the *graph canvas*.

Inspector Area: Inspectors are used to show and modify the properties of a process and its components. Figure 2 shows the *Service Logic Graph* (SLG) inspector that allows to drag&drop common resources – called *context variables* – on activities in order to define data dependencies in the model, set the name and package, as well as to define the compatibility to a specific input/output parameterization denoted by *graph interface*.

Graph Canvas: On the canvas, activities are arranged representing services and sub-processes. A modeler is able to connect them via named edges – called *branches* – in order to define the control-flow. This is the main area where an application expert can model workflows. Figure 2 shows a process that retrieves a collection of membership queries that are processed in a loop and eventually returned to a learning algorithm.

An in-depth explanation of the concepts and paradigms of *jABC4* can be found in [27, 28] and online on the project website,[5] where a dedicated installer is provided for download.

5   LearnLib Studio

Next generation LearnLib (NGLL) [24] was the precursor of the open-source *LearnLib* that used the approach of active automata learning together with the approach of service-oriented design and development of applications with the *jABC3* [38] to enable users to create learning solutions even without (or with little) programming skills.

The previous version of *LearnLib Studio* has already been used by undergraduate students in lectures on modern web technologies in 2013. It was employed to assist the students in testing and learning an abstraction of a self-implemented

---

[5] http://hope.scce.info.

web application, using the frontend testing technology of the *Selenium frame-work*.[6] *LearnLib Studio* was based on the aforementioned closed-source version of *LearnLib* and the *jABC3*, which both have been improved significantly, as has been outlined in the preceding sections. This lead to the decision to re-implement *LearnLib Studio* from scratch. In 2014, we extended our lecture to use our open-source version of *LearnLib*, and used it to learn models of REST services. *LearnLib Studio* further could be used by testers without programming skills like risk-analysts [39].

LearnLib Studio contains a large set of services as well as reusable processes (i.e., introducing hierarchical process modeling) to apply active automata learn-ing in different environments. This configurable and extensible library includes components for

- the usage of different learning algorithms like L_M^* [11] or TTT [17]
- the visualization of intermediate and final hypothesis automata
- the visualization of internal data structures for different algorithms (e.g., observation tables and discrimination trees)
- collecting statistics like processed membership or equivalence queries.

5.1   Rich Process Modeling

Most automata learning setups have a lot in common. For example, the iterative two-phase approach of hypothesis construction and equivalence testing, the use of a filter chain for runtime optimization, and the collection and presentation of statistical data are recurring patterns. These commonalities are exploited by *LearnLib Studio* by allowing a user to create reusable learning setups easily, to adapt a learning setup locally, as well as to combine the aspects of a learning setup (i.e., algorithm, alphabet, filter chain, equivalence oracle, ...) to a rich set of learning setup variants seamlessly. Technically, the key to this composi-tional process modeling is the HOPE [26] approach with its higher-order process passing, where generic processes can be parameterized dynamically with custom behavior defining the variation.

We describe the benefit of applying rich process modeling via an example taken from a tutorial contained in the *LearnLib Studio* distribution. Figure 3 shows a simple process that starts a local *Jetty* web server[7] from a configured predefined example, then proceeds to configure a learning algorithm with a test driver and predefined alphabet, and then starts learning an abstraction of a REST service running on the web server. Finally, the learned hypothesis automa-ton as well as the internal data structures of the chosen algorithm are displayed and the web server is stopped.

The service "*ProcessQueries*", depicted in Fig. 3, shows a realization of one of the main features of *jABC4* in *LearnLib Studio*: *generic higher-order process execution*. The small green overlay icon with a white star in the lower left corner

---

[6] http://www.seleniumhq.org/.
[7] http://eclipse.org/jetty/.

of the icon of the activity *"ProcessQueries"* marks it as a *constructor graph*, i.e., it creates a new process instance that can be passed to other processes *just like data*, instead of directly executing a sub process. In our new version of *LearnLib Studio*, the process *"Learning loop"* takes as input parameter a graph instance that implements the generic graph interface *"ProcessQueries"*. Each process implementing this graph interface can be used in a type-safe manner as input. For instance, the service graph depicted in Fig. 2 can be used as a concrete implementation, since it implements *"ProcessQueries"*. This is shown in the inspector on the bottom left in the component headed "Interfaces". This approach allows to dynamically exchange processes at runtime and therefore reduces the effort to implement variant-rich applications [26].

Fig. 3. Process for inferring a REST service from a web application.

5.2 Domain Tailoring

An exhaustive service library can become overwhelming and hard to manage for users. Additionally, the terminology and expertise differs between domains. Therefore, at some point the wish emerges to focus on a specific domain. To support users of *LearnLib Studio*, we use the *preconfiguration* feature of *jABC4* [21].

A so-called preconfiguration graph allows to select a subset of the globally available components that will be available within the considered domain. The contained activities can be renamed, the package can be adapted and even the documentation can be changed or translated to a different language without changing the original activity or the underlying service or process model. Further on, it is possible to predefine the data dependencies an activity reads from and writes to. This allows users to focus on the control-flow instead of managing the data-flow, and avoids a lot of repetitive work, as the preconfigured activities may be reused.

Figure 4 shows a generic higher-order learning loop using an interface graph as input for processing queries (depicted through activity *"Process"*). The depicted process is a service-oriented version of the simple learning loop from Listing 1: After the learning algorithm is able to build a first hypothesis automaton (left part), the search and refinement phases are iterated until no further counterexample to the current hypothesis is found. Since *LearnLib* is able to process batches of queries (cf. [12]), the activity *"Retrieve"* will attempt to collect several queries to be processed at once. This processing is delegated to an implementation of the interface graph *"Process"*, which may process them sequentially or in parallel. Due to its generic nature, this process can be used as an implementation of process *"Learning loop"* in Fig. 3, but it can also be used as a loop to learn a model of totally different target systems.

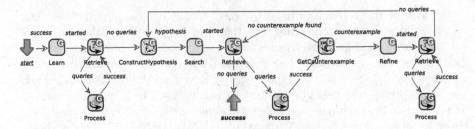

Fig. 4. Generic higher-order learning loop.

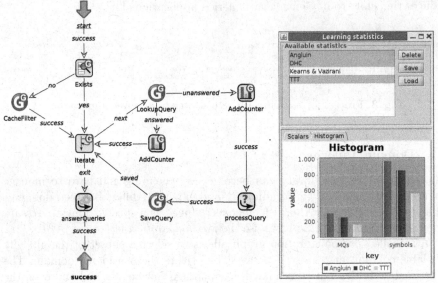

(a) Generic service implementation that uses a cache to avoid querying duplicate *MQs*

(b) Visualization of statistics for different algorithms

Fig. 5. *ProcessQueries* implementation and statistics visualization

An extended process implementation of the *"ProcessQueries"* interface graph enriched with services for collecting statistics is depicted in Fig. 5. Apart from the loop iterating over incoming queries, the process consists of a cache filter that stores the results of previous queries, avoiding duplicate queries being posed to the SUL. Depending on whether a query was forwarded to the SUL or could be answered by the cache, a configured counter will be incremented.

5.3 Visualization

To provide feedback from a learning process, *LearnLib Studio* allows to visualize hypothesis automata in the canvas without the necessity to install external tools. A service *"ShowJABCModel"* takes a hypothesis automaton (either

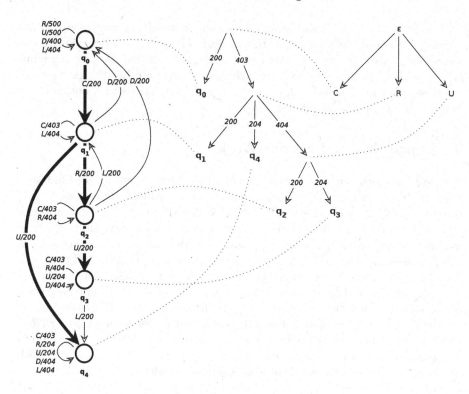

Fig. 6. Data structure of the TTT algorithm for the REST learning example.

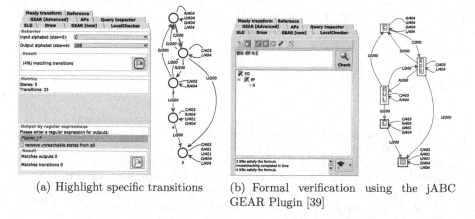

(a) Highlight specific transitions   (b) Formal verification using the jABC GEAR Plugin [39]

Fig. 7. Inspectors allow to interpret and change the semantics of models.

intermediate or final), and automatically layouts and displays a model. Internal data-structures may be visualized, like the *observation table* from Angluin-style algorithms, or from more sophisticated algorithms like TTT [17]. A visualized example data structure for the latter one is depicted in Fig. 6.

In addition to the visualization of hypothesis automata and internal data structures, *LearnLib Studio* is able to transform visualized Mealy machines into Kripke structures, model check them, and highlight transitions by selecting input or output symbols in order to show error paths, among other things. Furthermore, models can be simplified, e.g., by removing transitions with outputs that indicate failure of actions (cf. Fig. 7(a)).

6   Conclusion and Future Work

We have presented our new version of *LearnLib Studio*, a service-oriented approach to the execution and evaluation of learning experiments. Due to its generic service library, available example Mealy machines, in-place visualization facilities, and a set of tutorials, *LearnLib Studio* provides an easy entry to active automata learning applications. Based on the simplicity-oriented process modeling framework *jABC4*, a user neither needs to write a single line of code, nor does he or she need to understand the theoretical and technical foundation.

Learning a model from a real system currently requires an implementation of the alphabet and the corresponding test driver in *LearnLib Studio*. In [30], we already created the alphabet and a specific test driver from a set of *jABC4* processes that are generated to type-safe code, and used *LearnLib* to learn models of these processes. The next step would be to combine both approaches, which would allow to model and execute the complete model inference approach in *LearnLib Studio*.

In future versions, we would also like to use the *dependency injection* feature of *jABC4*, which allows to inject required variables or graph instances into a process without the need to specify them as process input when they are used. This would minimize the required parameter passing and therefore ease the usage.

References

1. Activiti Team: Activiti BPM Platform (2012). http://www.activiti.org/
2. Angluin, D.: Learning regular sets from queries and counterexamples. Inf. Comput. **75**(2), 87–106 (1987)
3. Bauer, O., Neubauer, J., Steffen, B., Howar, F.: Reusing system states by active learning algorithms. In: Moschitti, A., Scandariato, R. (eds.) EternalS 2011. CCIS, vol. 255, pp. 61–78. Springer, Heidelberg (2012). doi:10.1007/978-3-642-28033-7_6
4. Bollig, B., Habermehl, P., Kern, C., Leucker, M.: Angluin-style learning of NFA. In: IJCAI 2009, pp. 1004–1009. Morgan Kaufmann Publishers Inc., San Francisco (2009)
5. Bollig, B., Katoen, J.-P., Kern, C., Leucker, M., Neider, D., Piegdon, D.R.: libalf: the automata learning framework. In: Touili, T., Cook, B., Jackson, P. (eds.) CAV 2010. LNCS, vol. 6174, pp. 360–364. Springer, Heidelberg (2010). doi:10.1007/978-3-642-14295-6_32
6. Chow, T.S.: Testing software design modeled by finite-state machines. IEEE Trans. Softw. Eng. **4**(3), 178–187 (1978)

7. Clarke Jr., E.M., Grumberg, O., Peled, D.A.: Model Checking. MIT Press, Cambridge (1999)
8. Cobleigh, J.M., Giannakopoulou, D., PǍsǍreanu, C.S.: Learning assumptions for compositional verification. In: Garavel, H., Hatcliff, J. (eds.) TACAS 2003. LNCS, vol. 2619, pp. 331–346. Springer, Heidelberg (2003). doi:10.1007/3-540-36577-X_24
9. Dadam, P., et al.: From ADEPT to AristaFlow BPM suite: a research vision has become reality. In: Rinderle-Ma, S., Sadiq, S., Leymann, F. (eds.) BPM 2009. LNBIP, vol. 43, pp. 529–531. Springer, Heidelberg (2010). doi:10.1007/978-3-642-12186-9_50
10. Esparza, J., Leucker, M., Schlund, M.: Learning workflow petri nets. In: Lilius, J., Penczek, W. (eds.) PETRI NETS 2010. LNCS, vol. 6128, pp. 206–225. Springer, Heidelberg (2010). doi:10.1007/978-3-642-13675-7_13
11. Hagerer, A., Hungar, H., Niese, O., Steffen, B.: Model generation by moderated regular extrapolation. In: Kutsche, R.-D., Weber, H. (eds.) FASE 2002. LNCS, vol. 2306, pp. 80–95. Springer, Heidelberg (2002). doi:10.1007/3-540-45923-5_6
12. Howar, F., Bauer, O., Merten, M., Steffen, B., Margaria, T.: The teachers' crowd: the impact of distributed oracles on active automata learning. In: Hähnle, R., Knoop, J., Margaria, T., Schreiner, D., Steffen, B. (eds.) ISoLA 2011 Workshops. CCIS, vol. 336, pp. 232–247. Springer, Heidelberg (2012). doi:10.1007/978-3-642-34781-8_18
13. Howar, F., Isberner, M., Steffen, B.: Tutorial: automata learning in practice. In: Margaria, T., Steffen, B. (eds.) ISoLA 2014. LNCS, vol. 8802, pp. 499–513. Springer, Heidelberg (2014). doi:10.1007/978-3-662-45234-9_34
14. Hungar, H., Niese, O., Steffen, B.: Domain-specific optimization in automata learning. In: Hunt, W.A., Somenzi, F. (eds.) CAV 2003. LNCS, vol. 2725, pp. 315–327. Springer, Heidelberg (2003). doi:10.1007/978-3-540-45069-6_31
15. Irfan, M.N., Oriat, C., Groz, R.: Angluin style finite state machine inference with non-optimal counterexamples. In: Proceedings of the First International Workshop on Model Inference in Testing, MIIT 2010, pp. 11–19. ACM, New York (2010)
16. Isberner, M., Howar, F., Steffen, B.: Learning register automata: from languages to program structures. Mach. Learn. **96**(1–2), 65–98 (2014)
17. Isberner, M., Howar, F., Steffen, B.: The TTT algorithm: a redundancy-free approach to active automata learning. In: Bonakdarpour, B., Smolka, S.A. (eds.) RV 2014. LNCS, vol. 8734, pp. 307–322. Springer, Heidelberg (2014). doi:10.1007/978-3-319-11164-3_26
18. Isberner, M., Howar, F., Steffen, B.: The open-source LearnLib. In: Kroening, D., Pǎsǎreanu, C.S. (eds.) CAV 2015. LNCS, vol. 9206, pp. 487–495. Springer, Heidelberg (2015). doi:10.1007/978-3-319-21690-4_32
19. Isberner, M., Steffen, B.: An abstract framework for counterexample analysis in active automata learning. In: Clark, A., Kanazawa, M., Yoshinaka, R. (eds.) Proceedings of the 12th International Conference on Grammatical Inference, ICGI 2014, JMLR Proceedings, Kyoto, Japan, 17–19 September 2014, vol. 34, pp. 79–93 (2014). JMLR.org
20. Kearns, M.J., Vazirani, U.V.: An Introduction to Computational Learning Theory. MIT Press, Cambridge (1994)
21. Kühn, D., Neubauer, J.: Guided domain-specific tailoring of jABC4. In: Lamprecht, A.-L. (ed.) ISoLA 2012/2014. CCIS, vol. 683, pp. 113–127. Springer, Heidelberg (2016)
22. Margaria, T., Steffen, B.: Agile IT: thinking in user-centric models. In: Margaria, T., Steffen, B. (eds.) ISoLA 2008. CCIS, vol. 17, pp. 490–502. Springer, Heidelberg (2008). doi:10.1007/978-3-540-88479-8_35

23. Margaria, T., Steffen, B.: Service-orientation: conquering complexity with XMDD. In: Hinchey, M., Coyle, L. (eds.) Conquering Complexity, pp. 217–236. Springer, London (2012)

24. Merten, M., Steffen, B., Howar, F., Margaria, T.: Next generation LearnLib. In: Abdulla, P.A., Leino, K.R.M. (eds.) TACAS 2011. LNCS, vol. 6605, pp. 220–223. Springer, Heidelberg (2011). doi:10.1007/978-3-642-19835-9_18

25. Naujokat, S., Neubauer, J., Lamprecht, A.-L., Steffen, B., Jörges, S., Margaria, T.: Simplicity-first model-based plug-in development. Softw.: Pract. Exp. **44**(3), 277–297 (2014)

26. Neubauer, J.: Higher-order process engineering. Ph.D. thesis, Technische Universität, Dortmund (2014)

27. Neubauer, J., Steffen, B.: Plug-and-play higher-order process integration. Computer **46**(11), 56–62 (2013)

28. Neubauer, J., Steffen, B.: Second-order servification. In: Herzwurm, G., Margaria, T. (eds.) ICSOB 2013. LNBIP, vol. 150, pp. 13–25. Springer, Heidelberg (2013). doi:10.1007/978-3-642-39336-5_2

29. Neubauer, J., Steffen, B., Bauer, O., Windmüller, S., Merten, M., Margaria, T., Howar, F.: Automated continuous quality assurance. In: FormSERA 2012, pp. 37–43. IEEE Press, Piscataway (2012)

30. Neubauer, J., Windmüller, S., Steffen, B.: Risk-based testing via active continuous quality control. Int. J. Softw. Tools Technol. Transfer **16**(5), 569–591 (2014)

31. OMG: Business Process Model and Notation (BPMN) Version 2.0 (2011). http://www.omg.org/spec/BPMN/2.0/

32. RedHat Software - JBoss: jBPM Website (2012) http://www.jboss.org/jbpm

33. Rivest, R.L., Schapire, R.E.: Inference of finite automata using homing sequences. In: STOC 1989, pp. 411–420. ACM, New York (1989)

34. Robillard, M., Bodden, E., Kawrykow, D., Mezini, M., Ratchford, T.: Automated API property inference techniques. IEEE Trans. Software Eng. **39**(5), 613–637 (2013)

35. Sametinger, J.: Software Engineering with Reusable Components. Springer, New York (1997)

36. Shahbaz, M., Groz, R.: Inferring mealy machines. In: Cavalcanti, A., Dams, D.R. (eds.) FM 2009. LNCS, vol. 5850, pp. 207–222. Springer, Heidelberg (2009). doi:10.1007/978-3-642-05089-3_14

37. Steffen, B., Howar, F., Merten, M.: Introduction to active automata learning from a practical perspective. In: Bernardo, M., Issarny, V. (eds.) SFM 2011. LNCS, vol. 6659, pp. 256–296. Springer, Heidelberg (2011). doi:10.1007/978-3-642-21455-4_8

38. Steffen, B., Margaria, T., Nagel, R., Jörges, S., Kubczak, C.: Model-driven development with the jABC. In: Bin, E., Ziv, A., Ur, S. (eds.) HVC 2006. LNCS, vol. 4383, pp. 92–108. Springer, Heidelberg (2007). doi:10.1007/978-3-540-70889-6_7

39. Windmüller, S., Neubauer, J., Steffen, B., Howar, F., Bauer, O.: Active continuous quality control. In: Proceedings of the 16th International ACM Sigsoft Symposium on Component-Based Software Engineering, CBSE 2013, pp. 111–120. ACM, New York (2013)

40. Withers, D., Kawas, E., McCarthy, L., Vandervalk, B., Wilkinson, M.: Semantically-guided workflow construction in Taverna: the SADI and BioMoby plug-ins. In: Margaria, T., Steffen, B. (eds.) ISoLA 2010. LNCS, vol. 6415, pp. 301–312. Springer, Heidelberg (2010). doi:10.1007/978-3-642-16558-0_26

Counterexample-Guided Prefix Refinement Analysis for Program Verification

Marc Jasper[(✉)]

TU Dortmund University, 44221 Dortmund, Germany
marc.jasper@cs.tu-dortmund.de

Abstract. Counterexample-guided abstraction refinement (CEGAR) has become a successful approach to the automatic verification of program properties. Starting from a coarse abstract model, CEGAR incrementally refines the model based on spurious counterexamples that are retrieved from model checking attempts. In addition to purely symbolic representations of program states, recent work shows that a combination of an explicit-value and an abstract domain can be beneficial for CEGAR approaches. This paper introduces the counterexample-guided prefix refinement analysis (CEGPRA) that is based on the CEGAR idea and features a purely path-based model refinement. A first evaluation based on benchmarks from the rigorous examination of reactive systems (RERS) challenge indicates that CEGPRA is useful for analyzing a subset of temporal properties on large-scale reactive systems.

1 Introduction

Model checking has become a well-known approach to the automatic verification of program properties [1]. In addition, advances in model checking can help to improve the performance of data-flow analyses [14]. Despite its success, the *state explosion problem* presents a significant challenge to model checking [7,8].

Abstraction has been shown to be a powerful tool to ameliorate the state explosion problem [4,6]. The aim is to only inspect certain information about a program that suffices to prove the desired set of properties. Counterexample-guided abstraction refinement (CEGAR) [6] incrementally refines a coarse abstract model of the analyzed program automatically. Due to the abstract nature of such a model, its states are commonly represented symbolically by predicate constraints [6]. Recent work indicates that a CEGAR approach based on an explicit-value domain for a subset of the program's variables can be useful for automatic verification [4]. Because of expensive operations on the symbolic values of abstract states, storing explicit values for some states or variables can improve the performance of an analysis.

This paper introduces the CEGPRA algorithm that verifies *bounded temporal properties* on programs with a finite set of input values. The CEGPRA algorithm differs from traditional CEGAR approaches as it does not employ symbolic algorithms.

© Springer International Publishing AG 2016
A.-L. Lamprecht (Ed.): ISoLA 2012/2014, CCIS 683, pp. 143–155, 2016.
DOI: 10.1007/978-3-319-51641-7_9

Following this introduction, Sect. 2 is going to clarify the context of this paper by presenting related work. Section 3 introduces relevant preliminaries. The CEG-PRA algorithm is presented in Sect. 4 and illustrated by an analysis of reactive systems in Sect. 5. Afterwards, Sect. 6 evaluates CEGPRA by comparing it to the winning approach of the RERS'14 challenge. Section 7 presents a conclusion and an outlook to future work.

2 Related Work

Counterexample-guided abstraction refinement (CEGAR) [6] aims to analyze whether or not a temporal property holds on a given program. It refines an initial abstract model based on information extracted from spurious counterexamples. CEGAR has been introduced in the setting of an explicit-value analysis [4] and integrated in a framework that combines explicit-value and symbolic domains [3]. This existing approach refines abstract states.

Bounded model checking (BMC) [7] validates an analyzed property up to a given depth k of steps in the program's execution. BMC benefits from the efficient heuristics of SAT solvers.

The *rigorous examination of reactive systems* (RERS)[1] challenge provides participants with large-scale reactive systems and the task to analyze the correctness of related behavioral specifications [9]. The procedure used to automatically generate these systems allows the organizers to adjust a variety of characteristics that can pose a challenge to verification tools [15].

In the past, participants have used different approaches in order to analyze the RERS problems. The applied techniques involve explicit state model checking [12], concrete symbolic model checking [13], binary decision diagram (BDD)-based symbolic model checking [5], symbolic bounded model checking [11] and active automata learning [2]. The large scale of the given systems motivated several participants to apply an initial optimization or analysis in the form of state compression [12,13], precompilation [13] or a domain-type analysis [5].

Satisfiability modulo theories (SMT) solvers answer queries specified in a logic that extends boolean algebra. They delegate parts of the required reasoning to SAT solvers. SMT solvers can experience difficulties in handling the large-scale systems of RERS due to the size of the formulas that need to be processed [5].

3 Preliminaries

Kripke Structures. For the purpose of model checking, programs are frequently represented as Kripke structures. Let AP be a set of atomic propositions. A *Kripke structure* is a quadruple $M = (S, S_0, R, L)$ with the following characteristics:

- S is a set of states
- $S_0 \subseteq S$, the set of initial states

---

[1] http://www.rers-challenge.org/.

- $R : S \times S$ is a left-total transition relation, meaning $\forall s \in S \, \exists t \in S : (s,t) \in R$
- $L : S \to 2^{AP}$, a labeling function that maps each state $s \in S$ to a set of atomic propositions

If the set of initial states S_0 only contains a single element, the notation s_0 might be used instead.

Propositional Linear Temporal Logic (PLTL). Let AP be a set of atomic propositions and $a \in AP$. The syntax of PLTL is defined using the following Backus-Naur form [1]:

$$\phi ::= true \mid a \mid \phi_1 \wedge \phi_2 \mid \neg\phi \mid X(\phi) \mid \phi_1 \text{ U } \phi_2$$

The operator X (or "next") describes behavior that has to hold at the next time step. The formula ϕ_1 U ϕ_2 (or ϕ_1 "until" ϕ_2) describes that ϕ_2 has to occur eventually and that ϕ_1 has to hold until ϕ_2 occurs in the sequence.

Operators for frequently occurring meanings include $F(\phi):=(true \text{ U } \phi)$ for finally and its dual operator $G(\phi):=\neg(F(\neg\phi))$ for generally. Additional operators such as disjunction, implication and equivalence can be derived just like in boolean algebra. The example in this paper also uses the weak-until operator WU: $(\phi_1 \text{ WU } \phi_2) := (\phi_1 \text{ U } \phi_2) \vee G(\phi_1)$. The terms LTL and PLTL are used interchangeably within the scope of this paper.

4   Counterexample-Guided Prefix Refinement Analysis

CEGPRA aims to verify a property on an over-approximating program model. After each unsuccessful model checking attempt, CEGPRA refines the model based on information extracted from a spurious counterexample. The analysis therefore follows the idea of an iterative refinement found in CEGAR approaches. A single refinement step excludes the most recent spurious counterexample. Within each refinement step, CEGPRA prepends a path of concrete states to the model in a way so that the resulting model still over-approximates the analyzed program. Analyzing a prefix of concrete states resembles BMC, but only leads to correct results within the CEGPRA algorithm. The type of refinement applied by CEGPRA differs from CEGAR approaches which subdivide the abstract states in the model.

Target Properties. The subset of properties that CEGPRA can analyze efficiently contains *bounded temporal properties*. CEGPRA's model refinement can be seen as a localized unrolling of the analyzed program's state space. This choice limits the category of temporal properties that CEGPRA can analyze efficiently. Target properties contain *bounded liveness properties* that are satisfied if a desirable condition occurs a finite number of times and/or *bounded safety properties* that are satisfied if they hold within an initial boundary condition. A simple example of a bounded safety property is an ATM that is not allowed to dispense money before the user enters his or her credit card and authorization code.

The information represented by the initial abstract model is a key ingredient to the CEGPRA approach as it constrains the set of potentially feasible program executions. By only unrolling the concrete state space where the initial abstract model is too coarse, CEGPRA can yield a smaller model than a simple exploration of the reachable state space. When analyzing compound properties, CEGPRA can verify desired characteristics that cannot be derived using exhaustive search only. As an example, assume that the initial abstract model suffices to infer parts of the property that have to hold throughout the entire program (safety properties). In the case of additional constraints on the early stages of program executions, CEGPRA's refinement can verify these additional sub-properties.

Initial Abstract Model. The path-based prefix refinement of CEGPRA is compatible with various initial abstract models. For an analyzed program with the concrete Kripke structure $M = (S, s_0, R, L)$, any model $\hat{M} = (\hat{S}, \hat{s}_0, \hat{R}, \hat{L})$ fulfilling the following criteria can be refined by the algorithm:

- $\hat{M}$ over-approximates M
- There exists a function $h : S \to \hat{S}$ that partitions S
- $\forall s \in S \, \forall s_1, s_2 \in R(s) : s_1 \neq s_2 \implies h(s_1) \neq h(s_2)$

The first requirement is necessary in order to allow for a verification without false positives. The second constraint guarantees that states which are represented by existing abstract states can be prepended without introducing additional paths. The third condition ensures that each path in the abstract model maps to exactly one execution path in the analyzed program. This eliminates the need for treating counterexample paths symbolically. At the same time, the resulting size of the initial abstraction restricts the CEGPRA approach to programs with a finite and comparably small range of input values.

CEGPRA Algorithm. Algorithm 1 presents the CEGPRA approach in detail. For related proofs, refer to [10]. CEGPRA maintains a set of transitions T that link concrete and abstract states in the model $\hat{M}$. T is initialized accordingly (line 1). During each iteration of the CEGPRA loop, the transitions in T are removed from the model (line 5) before the most recent counterexample ce retrieved from model checking is analyzed (line 7). Procedure $traceAndCompare$ therefore only observes the concrete states in $\hat{M}$ when it compares ce to the real program semantics.

Procedure $traceAndCompare$ initially resets the output parameters T_{new} and S_{new} to empty sets. It extracts the input sequence of ce and uses it to step-wise trace the analyzed program. The observable behavior of each program state discovered this way is compared to the corresponding abstract state's behavior in the counterexample trace. $traceAndCompare$ terminates when the observable behaviors contradict each other (spurious counterexample) or when a cycle of concrete states is detected (real counterexample). Newly discovered states and transitions are inserted into the sets S_{new} and T_{new} respectively. The real execution path explored by $traceAndCompare$ is integrated into the model $\hat{M}$, more precisely into its prefix of concrete states. This guarantees that the same spurious counterexample will not be reported twice.

CEGPRA

Input: initial abstract model: $\hat{M} = (\hat{S}, \hat{s}_0, \hat{R}, \hat{L})$
Input: partitioning abstraction function $h : S \rightarrow \hat{S}$
Input: target property and set of all analyzed properties: (p, P)
Input: concrete start state of the analyzed system: s_0
Output: analysis results for each property: P_{res}

1: $T \leftarrow \{(s_p, \hat{s}_a) \mid (s_p, \hat{s}_a) \in \hat{R} \wedge |s_p| = 1 \wedge |\hat{s}_a| > 1\}$
2: $recentRes \leftarrow \text{modelCheck}(\hat{M}, p)$
3: $\hat{s}_0 \leftarrow s_0$
4: **while** $recentRes.value \neq$ "verified" **do**
5:     $\hat{R} \leftarrow \hat{R} - T$
6:     Counterexample $ce \leftarrow recentRes.witness$
7:     $realCe \leftarrow \text{traceAndCompare}(ce, \hat{M}, T_{new}, S_{new})$
8:     **if** $realCe$ **then**
9:         **break**
10:     $T \leftarrow \text{updateLinkingTransitions}(T, h, T_{new}, S_{new})$
11:     $\hat{R} \leftarrow \hat{R} \cup T$
12:     $recentRes \leftarrow \text{modelCheck}(\hat{M}, p)$
13: **return**$(\{(p, recentRes.value)\} \cup \text{tryToVerifyAllProperties}(\hat{M}, (P - \{p\})))$

Algorithm 1: CEGPRA. Aims to analyze a property $p \in P$ by refining an abstract program model $\hat{M}$ based on history information.

    Function *updateLinkingTransitions* serves the following purpose: Reconnect every concrete state s_p using outgoing transitions as if it would be the corresponding abstract state $h(s_p)$, except for where a transition to a concrete successor state of s_p exists. This results in an over-approximating model $\hat{M}$ at line 12 of Algorithm 1.

    CEGPRA returns a set of analysis results which includes that of target property p. In addition, procedure *tryToVerifyAllProperties* contributes all those properties and their respective results that are verifiable using the refined abstract model $\hat{M}$.

5   Analyzing Reactive Systems Using CEGPRA

This section illustrates the CEGPRA algorithm on an exemplary program. CEGPRA is used to verify a property on the reactive system "Problem 3"[2] that was part of the RERS'14 challenge. The 2014 iteration of RERS featured a white-box challenge. All of the RERS'14 problems including "Problem 3" consist of two parts: a reactive system in the form of auto-generated source code that is available in C and Java and a related specification file containing 100 LTL properties.

---

[2] http://www.rers-challenge.org/2014Isola/problems/WhiteBox/Problem3/Problem
3.c.

Analyzed System. All RERS challenge programs represent *event-condition-action* (ECA) systems. These systems can be described as looping through event-triggered cycles. In the case of the RERS benchmarks, this cycle consists of input, internal computation and resulting output. RERS benchmarks contain deterministic ECA systems of finite size. An important characteristic is their comparably small input alphabet that does not exceed 20 distinct symbols. These systems further feature predefined initial assignments to variables and contain exit states where the program terminates. The supplied LTL properties only constrain the input-output behavior of infinite runs of the system. In the following notation, input symbols have an 'i' as a prefix or blue background. Output symbols are referred to by the prefix 'o' or orange background.

Example. The following example aims to verify that behavioral LTL property "#84"[3] holds on the system:

> **Property 84.** *Input D precedes output S, output V before input B* $\iff$
> $(G(\neg iB)) \vee ((iB \vee \neg oS \vee X(\neg oV \text{ WU } iB)) \text{ U } (iB \vee iD))$[4]

Looking at the automatically generated property 84, it becomes apparent that it is a disjunction of two subformulas. The second subformula is satisfied if a certain condition holds until either input symbol B or D is discovered on a given path. Due to existing exit states (marked as red circles in the illustrations), the number of paths reflecting input sequences without the symbols B and D might be small. The CEGPRA analysis of Algorithm 1 will discover these exit states, thereby refine the set of feasible paths and enable the model checker to verify property 84.

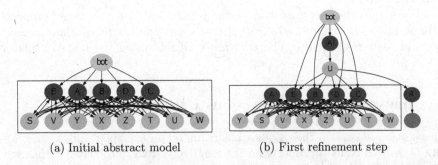

(a) Initial abstract model   (b) First refinement step

Fig. 1. CEGPRA example: Initial abstract model and first refinement step (Color figure online)

Figure 1a shows the initial abstract model. The heavily interconnected states in the outlined box represent the cluster of abstract states. The concrete start

---

[3] http://www.rers-challenge.org/2014Isola/problems/constraints-RERS14-5.txt.

[4] The syntax of the auto-generated LTL property 84 has been altered for this example without changing the semantics.

state is denoted as *bot* for bottom because no input or output event has occurred yet. A first model checking attempt yields a spurious counterexample path with the prefix $\langle iA, oU, iA, oS, iB \ldots \rangle$.

After disconnecting state *bot* from the abstract states (Algorithm 1, line 5), CEGPRA calls the procedure *traceAndCompare* (line 7) that analyzes the counterexample based on its input sequence. The first spurious transition occurs after the second input symbol: The concrete program semantics dictate an exit state after the second input iA (red circle in Fig. 1b), but the counterexample claims an output oS at this index. The real program trace is integrated into the prefix of concrete states by procedure *traceAndCompare*. After function *updateLinkingTransitions* reconnects concrete and abstract states in a manner that over-approximates the program's semantics (lines 10, 11), the first spurious counterexample is rendered unfeasible (see Fig. 1b).

The model is not yet describing the set of feasible I/O-paths precisely enough to allow for a verification of property 84. A second spurious counterexample starts with the prefix $\langle iE, oS, iB, \ldots \rangle$ as the loop in Algorithm 1 continues. Four additional refinement steps are required by CEGPRA in order to successfully verify property 84 (Figs. 2a–d).

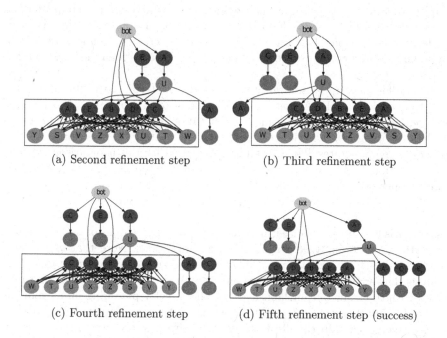

(a) Second refinement step

(b) Third refinement step

(c) Fourth refinement step

(d) Fifth refinement step (success)

Fig. 2. CEGPRA example: refinement steps 2–5

As can be seen in the resulting model (Fig. 2d), only abstract input states that represent input symbols B and D are reachable from concrete states after the five refinement steps. The model checker can now verify that the condition

(B ∨ ¬S ∨ X(¬V $W U$B)) holds before input B or D occurs on any infinite path that is feasible in the model. The attempted verification succeeds (Algorithm 1, line 12).

6   Evaluation of CEGPRA

This section presents a first evaluation of CEGPRA based on benchmarks from the RERS'14 challenge. The RERS problem sets feature large-scale ECA systems and are further described in Sect. 5. Each problem features 100 behavioral properties specified in LTL. The participant's task is to determine for each of the given properties whether or not it holds on the analyzed system. The large scale of the RERS benchmarks poses a challenge to current verification techniques.

Because the SMT solvers that are used by CEGAR approaches can struggle when analyzing the complex systems of RERS [5], the following evaluation compares CEGPRA to a different type of analysis that is called COMBINED within this paper. COMBINED was used by the winning participants of the RERS'14 challenge and also features the concept of prepending a prefix of concrete states to an abstract model. Instead of an iterative refinement based on counterexamples, COMBINED unrolls the analyzed system's concrete state space until a certain depth k of the ECA loop is reached. An over-approximating abstract model is then appended to the model in order to create a sound abstraction based on the concrete k-prefix of possible traces. For additional definitions refer to [10].

The following comparison always applies the analyses COMBINED and CEGPRA to the identical ECA system M. The same over-approximating model is used both as the initial abstract model of CEGPRA and as the appended abstract model of COMBINED. The single parameter of COMBINED is the depth k of the prefix of concrete states. The CEGPRA version used for this comparison expects as an additional input the maximum number of counterexamples c_{max} that are analyzed per property.

The comparison is based on the number of correctly analyzed properties and on the number of distinct I/O-states in each model as a tiebreaker. Computing less states is beneficial because it indicates that larger programs or more complex properties can be analyzed within resource limitations. Note that exit states and the input states directly preceding them are not stored explicitly by either analysis during the following evaluation. The abstract model contains multiple states with the same output label because the directly preceding input value is used to further characterize the state. Abstract states with the same output label are still merged within the illustrations. $|S_C|$ always represents the number of states in the model of CEGPRA after the analysis is finished. COMBINED discovers refutable properties before abstract states are appended to the model. When a property is proven false by COMBINED, the number of concrete states $|S_U|$ in the prefix is measured. For verified or unresolved properties, the comparison to CEGPRA is based on the total number of concrete and abstract states $|S_O|$ in the final model of COMBINED.

This evaluation is structured according to two different types of measurements. Section 6.1 compares CEGPRA and COMBINED based on the analysis of single properties. Section 6.2 presents results for the analysis of mixed sets of properties.

6.1   Analysis of Individual Properties

Measurements (Part 1). The following measurements are based on the analysis of all of the 100 behavioral LTL properties specified for "Problem 3", an ECA system from the RERS'14 challenge. The data regarding CEGPRA was gained by restarting the analysis for every single property, meaning the refinement from one property was not reused for analyzing a different one. The statistics for COMBINED represent the values related to the depth of the concrete-state prefix with which the property can be assessed for the first time. During these measurements, the maximum depth $k = 15$ was chosen for the COMBINED analysis. A maximum of $c_{max} = 500$ counterexamples was used for CEGPRA during this measurement because this maximum suffices for retrieving the same verification results as COMBINED. A detailed table of the results can be found in [10].

Results for Verified Properties. For the given data set and analysis limits, CEGPRA can assess the exact same subset of properties as COMBINED. When looking at the number of computed states $|S_C|$ and $|S_O|$, CEGPRA results in less states for each of the verified properties (see Fig. 3). Figure 4a illustrates the final model when analyzing property "#1" using CEGPRA. The model of COMBINED when analyzing the same property can be seen in Fig. 4b.

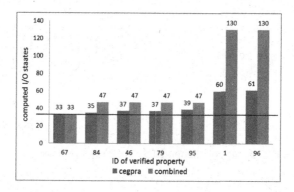

Fig. 3. Final size of the models for verified properties. The black line indicates the size of the initial abstraction.

Results for Disproved Properties. Within this measurement, all analyzed properties that do not hold on ECA system "Problem 3" are correctly identified by both analyses. Except for a single case, the presented CEGPRA algorithm requires the computation of more distinct states in order to yield a result (see

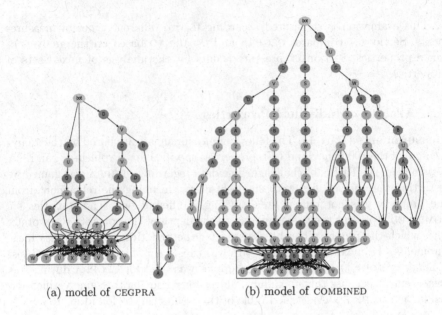

(a) model of CEGPRA   (b) model of COMBINED

Fig. 4. Final models of CEGPRA and COMBINED (verified LTL property "#1")

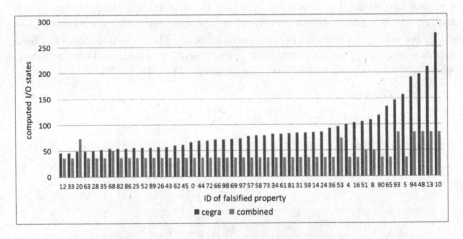

Fig. 5. Size of the model for disproved properties

Fig. 5). The higher number of states when using CEGPRA is based on two reasons. On the one hand, the 33 abstract states of the initial model are not included in the count for COMBINED because this analysis can disprove properties using just the prefix of concrete states. On the other hand, spurious counterexamples returned by the model checker are not always minimal with regard to the number of transitions until the first spurious behavior occurs.

Table 1. Analysis statistics of three properties only verified by CEGPRA

Property ID	Result cegpra	Distinct I/O states	Counterexamples
29	Yes	793	1274
55	Yes	756	945
60	Yes	774	1179

Measurements (Part 2). CEGPRA is now allowed to exceed the previous maximum of $c_{max} = 500$ counterexamples. Again, the analysis attempts to verify each of the 100 LTL properties specified for "Problem 3".

Results. CEGPRA successfully verifies three additional properties within the memory limit of the test machine (see Table 1). Even though up to more than 1000 counterexamples need to be analyzed, the final models contain less than 800 distinct I/O states due to exit-state branches that are not stored explicitly. One final model contains paths of 159 distinct I/O-states. COMBINED cannot verify these additional properties within the resource limitations. Due to 5 possible input values at the start of each iteration of the ECA loop, unrolling all concrete states potentially leads to a model of exponential size compared to its depth. COMBINED exceeds the memory use of the sufficient CEGPRA model after 23 of the required 159 loop iterations.

6.2   Analysis of Sets of Properties

Measurements. The following measurements again refer to "Problem 3" of the RERS'14 challenge. A modified version of CEGPRA called CEGPRA-MULTI is chosen here that reuses the refined model from one property to another. The order in which the 100 properties are analyzed is identical to the one found in the RERS challenge[5]. The threshold for analyzed counterexamples c_{max} still counts for each property individually and is set to $c_{max} = 100$. In order to compare CEGPRA-MULTI with COMBINED, the number of states $|S_O|$ in the final model of COMBINED is measured for all depths $i \in [0, k]_{\mathbb{N}_0}$ with $k = 23$.

Results for Verified Properties. Like in the previous evaluation using single properties, only CEGPRA can verify the three additional LTL properties shown in Table 1. During this measurement, all properties that are verified by both analyses are correctly assessed after computing 210 distinct I/O states by CEGPRA and after 130 states by COMBINED.

Results for Disproved Properties. Both analyses again refute all falsifiable properties. In order to disprove all of these properties, COMBINED requires the computation of 177 distinct I/O states corresponding to the first 8 loop iterations of the analyzed ECA system. CEGPRA-MULTI refutes some properties after computing more than 3000 distinct I/O states. Because of the over-approximating

---

[5] http://www.rers-challenge.org/2014Isola/problems/constraints-RERS14-5.txt.

model refined by CEGPRA, counterexamples might be spurious and therefore need to be checked before they are reported. CEGPRA only inspects counterexamples regarding the currently analyzed property. The refutation of later scheduled properties is therefore only attempted after the size of the model has been increased due to previous refinements.

7   Conclusion and Future Work

The CEGPRA algorithm introduced in this paper is similar to CEGAR approaches as it involves automated model refinements for the purpose of program verification. CEGPRA presents a useful alternative if handling symbolic representations becomes too complex. CEGPRA does not yield false positives and works without employing symbolic algorithms. The latter implies that no SMT solvers are required and also allows for a fast identification of real cyclic counterexamples [10]. The refinement within CEGPRA aims to verify properties and does not improve on a search for counterexamples when a property is refutable. While being theoretically complete for finite systems, CEGPRA is only efficient for the verification of properties that belong to the target category (see Sect. 4).

When compared to the analysis COMBINED that is also designed without utilizing symbolic algorithms, the counterexample-guided CEGPRA can verify a larger set of properties within resource limitations (see Sect. 6). COMBINED was used by the winning participants of the RERS'14 challenge. By verifying more properties than COMBINED, CEGPRA shows to be a useful analysis for the verification of certain temporal properties on large-scale reactive systems.

Future work should include a comparison of CEGPRA to a traditional CEGAR approach that refines abstract states. On the one hand, a traditional CEGAR algorithm is able to analyze a wider range of properties than CEGPRA if the analyzed system's size allows for symbolic reasoning. On the other hand, CEGPRA might analyze certain properties faster or could be applied in situations where SMT solvers are overwhelmed by the program's complexity. If CEGPRA shows to be a useful addition to traditional CEGAR approaches, it can be of interest to conceive an overall framework that is able to utilize both types of refinement.

References

1. Baier, C., Katoen, J.P., et al.: Principles of Model Checking, vol. 26202649. MIT Press, Cambridge (2008)
2. Bauer, O., Geske, M., Isberner, M.: Analyzing program behavior through active automata learning. Int. J. Softw. Tools Technol. Transfer 16(5), 531–542 (2014)
3. Beyer, D., Henzinger, T.A., Théoduloz, G.: Program analysis with dynamic precision adjustment. In: 23rd IEEE/ACM International Conference on Automated Software Engineering, ASE 2008, pp. 29–38. IEEE (2008)
4. Beyer, D., Löwe, S.: Explicit-state software model checking based on CEGAR and interpolation. In: Cortellessa, V., Varró, D. (eds.) FASE 2013. LNCS, vol. 7793, pp. 146–162. Springer, Heidelberg (2013). doi:10.1007/978-3-642-37057-1_11

5. Beyer, D., Stahlbauer, A.: BDD-based software verification. Applications to event-condition-action systems. Int. J. Softw. Tools Technol. Transfer **16**(5), 507–518 (2014)
6. Clarke, E.M., Grumberg, O., Jha, S., Lu, Y., Veith, H.: Counterexample-guided abstraction refinement for symbolic model checking. J. ACM **50**(5), 752–794 (2003)
7. Clarke, E., Biere, A., Raimi, R., Zhu, Y.: Bounded model checking using satisfiability solving. Formal Methods Syst. Des. **19**(1), 7–34 (2001)
8. Dams, D., Grumberg, O., Gerth, R.: Generation of reduced models for checking fragments of CTL. In: Courcoubetis, C. (ed.) CAV 1993. LNCS, vol. 697, pp. 479–490. Springer, Heidelberg (1993). doi:10.1007/3-540-56922-7_39
9. Howar, F., Isberner, M., Merten, M., Steffen, B., Beyer, D., Pasareanu, C.S.: Rigorous examination of reactive systems. The RERS challenges 2012 and 2013. Int. J. Softw. Tools Technol. Transfer **16**(5), 457–464 (2014)
10. Jasper, M.: Counterexample-guided abstraction refinement for the verification of large-scale reactive systems. Bachelor thesis, TU Dortmund University (2015)
11. Morse, J., Cordeiro, L., Nicole, D., Fischer, B.: Applying symbolic bounded model checking to the 2012 RERS greybox challenge. Int. J. Softw. Tools Technol. Transfer **16**(5), 519–529 (2014)
12. van de Pol, J., Ruys, T.C., te Brinke, S.: Thoughtful brute-force attack of the RERS 2012 and 2013 challenges. Int. J. Softw. Tools Technol. Transfer **16**(5), 481–491 (2014)
13. Schordan, M., Prantl, A.: Combining static analysis and state transition graphs for verification of event-condition-action systems in the RERS 2012 and 2013 challenges. Int. J. Softw. Tools Technol. Transfer **16**(5), 493–505 (2014)
14. Steffen, B.: Data flow analysis as model checking. In: Ito, T., Meyer, A.R. (eds.) TACS 1991. LNCS, vol. 526, pp. 346–364. Springer, Heidelberg (1991). doi:10.1007/3-540-54415-1_54
15. Steffen, B., Isberner, M., Naujokat, S., Margaria, T., Geske, M.: Property-driven benchmark generation: synthesizing programs of realistic structure. Int. J. Softw. Tools Technol. Transfer **16**(5), 465–479 (2014)

Author Index

Printed in the United States
By Bookmasters